CIRCULAR WALKS
IN THE BLACK MOUNTAINS

Circular Walks in the Black Mountains

Nick Jenkins

GWASG Carreg Gwalch

ISBN: 0-86381-558-8

Cover photo: Nick Jenkins

Cover design: Alan Jones

First published in 1999 by
Gwasg Carreg Gwalch, 12 Iard yr Orsaf, Llanrwst, Wales LL26 0EH
☎ 01492 642031   📠 01492 641502
✆ books@carreg-gwalch.co.uk   Web site: www.carreg-gwalch.co.uk

Circular Walks in the Black Mountains

If you thought you knew the Black Mountains, this handy pocket sized walking guide might just prove you wrong! Tucked away on the border between Wales and England, this is an area that has jealously guarded her secrets from walkers. But pry into those secrets and you'll discover a true paradise of long, high 'striding' ridges and deep green valleys, crying out to be explored and unearthed.

This book presents a lively potted history and geography of the area to add interest to your walking adventures. Also included are some of the local lores and tales, supplying that magical ingredient to really make you want to go and see for yourself just what might be lying in wait out there.

Each walk gives clear and concise directions, checked for accuracy by fellow walkers, and is accompanied by a sketch map. In addition, points of interest along the way are highlighted on the map, and written about after the walk description.

Attractions in the Black Mountains include ancient tombs, fascinating medieval churches, nature reserves, lovely country pubs, and some of the best and most sustained ridge walking to be found anywhere (three of the walks take in stretches of the Offa's Dyke Path). So pick up this book, put your boots on and let's go!

About the Author

Nick Jenkins is a keen walker and landscape photographer, having walked extensively both at home and abroad. His favourite and most often tramped areas are the Lake District, North Wales, the Yorkshire Dales, Pembrokeshire and the Brecon Beacons. He has also walked as far afield as the French Alps, Kashmir and Nepal, with his brother-in-law. His first walking book, 'Circular Walks in Gower', is also published by Gwasg Carreg Gwalch.

Nick has contributed a number of walks to walking magazines including 'High' and 'Country Walking'. A number of the walks in this book have previously appeared in 'Country Walking'.

Contents

Acknowledgements

The preparation of this book has eaten into my spare time with a voracious appetite for about a year. It has been a real labour of love even when bending against wind and rain, high up on an exposed ridge, to meet deadlines. I have walked and photographed pretty well all of the National Park and approached this project with a misplaced sense of deja vu. Boy, was I wrong. The research, not only for the walks but also for some of the more interesting titbits along the way, has brought me in touch with places I never knew existed!

The production of the final manuscript has been greatly helped by the assistance and kindness of local people who have stopped to chat and pass on useful snippets of information which I, in turn, have been able to pass on to you. In particular, however, I would like to extend my gratitude to the following:

Kate Carr, Public Relations Officer for the National Park, for so cheerfully checking references to Park information for accuracy; Sue Mabberly (Park Head Warden), Mike Scruby and Clive Williams (Park Wardens), for checking out the legality of rights of way; Phillip Park of the National Trust for information on areas under the Trust's ownership or custody; Colin and Daphne Gardiner of Gellirhyd Farm, Llangenny, for all sorts of interesting information on the area(and two bottles of their excellent home produced apple juice!) and, finally, to my wife, Anne, and my son, Stephen, for once more putting up with my disappearing acts (I never once got away with moaning about the hard work involved!).

Introduction

The Black Mountains (not to be confused with Mynydd Du [Black Mountain] to the west) are to be found in the eastern part of the Brecon Beacons National Park. They are separated from their high level cousins by the wide valley of the Usk, (or Wysg, in Welsh). They must have presented a formidable barrier either to prospective invaders of Wales, or (Heaven forbid) to the Welsh trying to escape from their native land. Along their lofty eastern escarpments runs the Offa's Dyke Path, an excellent long distance footpath which runs for the full length of Wales from Prestatyn to Chepstow, a distance of some 140 miles (about 225 kilometres). Strictly speaking the Black Mountains cross over the Welsh border at their extreme eastern edge and spill, just ever so slightly, over the boundary of the Park. Not to include this 'spillage' would constitute a nonsense, as it would omit some very fine walking and, besides, on the ground the boundary is completely invisible anyway!

The Black Mountains are no less challenging to the walker than their siblings to the west, and offer some superb and sustained ridge walking of a quality that is just crying out to be discovered. In between these finger-like ridges are deep valleys cloaked both in mystery and history; there are green valleys clothed in patchwork fields, and wooded slopes rich in wildlife and steeped in ancient lore. Here is an area that will amply repay detailed exploration, and how better to do so than by tugging on your boots, packing your rucksack, and striding out with a map and this companion for your guide?

The Brecon Beacons National Park (Parc Cenedlaethol Bannau Brycheiniog) divides fairly neatly into four distinct upland areas. From west to east, these are; Mynydd Du (Black Mountain), extending from Llandeilo to the minor road connecting the Upper Swansea Valley (Dyffryn Tawe) with Trecastell; Fforest Fawr, continuing east as far as the main A470 Cardiff to Brecon (Aberhonddu) road; the Central Beacons,

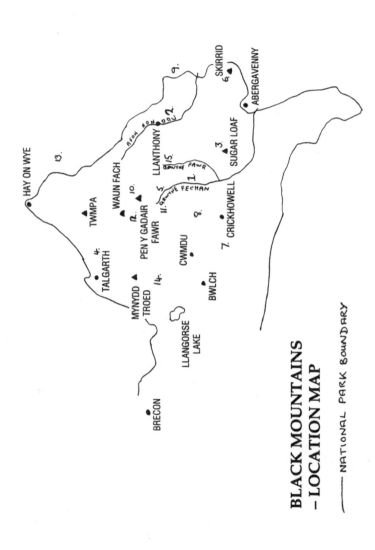

BLACK MOUNTAINS – LOCATION MAP

—— NATIONAL PARK BOUNDARY

10

running on to the Usk Valley (Dyffryn Wysg); and finally the Black Mountains, from the Usk Valley up to and just over the border into Herefordshire, and England. It is this last section that will be our home for the rest of this book.

National Park status was conferred on the Brecon Beacons, including the Black Mountains, in 1957. This special status has been a major factor in maintaining the rugged beauty of the area covered by the Park. Agriculture is the mainstay of the economy, with a not inconsiderable acreage being given over to common grazing. Tourism, whilst contributing significantly to the income of the area, plays very much a second fiddle to farming. Industry, mainly in the form of mineral extraction and iron smelting, certainly played a key role in the period from the 17th to the early 20th century, but pretty well all that now remains are the scars, in the form of quarries, tram roads and the odd ruin or two. To nature's credit, these scars have now started to meld with the countryside around them, and now present a strangely appealing beauty rather than their previous brutal ugliness.

The main towns lying within this area of the Park are Talgarth, Crickhowell and Hay-on-Wye (Y Gelli Gandryll), which is renowned for being the second-hand book capital of the world. Just outside the boundary of the Park lies the town of Abergavenny (Y Fenni), frequently referred to as the 'Gateway to the National Park'. This sleepy little town nestles in between the heights of the Sugar Loaf (Pen-y-fâl), 1,955 feet (596 metres), Skirrid Fawr 1,596 feet (486 metres) and Blorenge 1,833 feet (559 metres).

The Black Mountains are only crossed by one major road, the A479, which winds its way up the Rhiangoll valley to connect Crickhowell and Talgarth by way of Pengenffordd. To the east of the A479, minor 'No Through Roads' lead into the Grwyne Fechan and Grwyne Fawr valleys (pronounced locally as something like 'groiney'), and further east again a delightful (but in parts very narrow) road runs through the Vale of Ewyas alongside Afon Honddu, joining Llanfihangel Crucorney to

Hay-on-Wye. This latter road passes through the pretty hamlets of Llanthony (Llanddewi Nant Hodni) and Capel-y-ffin, about which more later. It then runs high over Bwlch yr Efengyl (the Gospel Pass), so named as it was a route taken by the Archbishop of Canterbury drumming up support for the crusades in the 12th century, accompanied by Gerallt Gymro (Giraldus Cambrensis). However, another tale tells of one of the daughters of Caratacus (Caradog in Welsh and Caractacus in Hollywood), leader of the Celtic Silures tribe around the time of the Roman occupation, inviting Saint Peter and Saint Paul to preach the Gospel to her people, and that this was the route they took. Up until comparatively recently this road was only fit for motor traffic as far as Llanthony. The stretch between Llanthony and Capel-y-ffin was, as late as 1913, 'somewhat narrow and rough' and from Capel-y-ffin over the Gospel Pass to Hay-on-Wye, passage was passable only by cart.

In terms of how best to explore the Black Mountains there is no shortage of places to base yourself, from both strategic and accommodation points of view. Abergavenny (Y Fenni) certainly offers a good base, with both hotels and B & Bs, and is within easy reach of a number of the walks contained in this guide. It also has the added advantage of being on the main Cardiff to Manchester railway line and is only about half an hour from Cardiff Central Station. Crickhowell, Talgarth and Hay-on-Wye also offer good accommodation. The National Park Information Centre (01874 623156) can supply further information on other suitable accommodation in the area.

The lanes in and around the Black Mountains are tortuously narrow and twisty, with high hedgebanks, and should be afforded every respect. More than once have I almost not made it to my chosen destination for that day; attempts to thwart me being cunningly executed by slow moving tractors, wide vans and horses. Be aware that this is real pony trekking country, and frequent use is made of the lanes for this popular pastime. Provided that they are in front of you and heading in the same direction, their imminent presence can usually be detected by familiar deposits on the tarmac. If, on the other hand, they are heading towards you, nothing is more disconcerting (for driver, rider and probably the horse) than a close encounter of the avoidable kind. Be warned and take care!

Given the aforementioned narrowness of the lanes hereabouts, and their potential for congestion and pollution, there is currently a concerted effort being made by the National Park Authority to encourage drivers to leave their cars at home (or wherever they are based), and to take advantage of local public transport. This comes under the 'Beacons Bus' initiative, the latest details of which are available from the National Park centres listed at the back of the book (or ring the National Park Information Centre on 01874 623156). Pick-up points include Hereford, Hay-on-Wye, Talgarth, Brecon, Abergavenny, Crickhowell and Bwlch. The scheme is fairly new but seems to make a lot of sense, and is well worth considering. It can also be used to great advantage, of course, if your wanderings lead you on to plan linear walks, starting from one end of a ridge and finishing at the other.

Brief History

To talk of the history of the Black Mountains in isolation from the rest of the National Park (or, to some extent, South Wales) is rather like offering a critique of the roast potatoes in a Sunday dinner, and ignoring the other contents on the plate. It can't be done. Neolithic Man, for example, didn't just confine his admiration of the area to this little corner; rather, he took in the full tour. However, for the purposes of keeping details relevant to our area I have outlined the local history only in terms of its impact here, and this in no way lacks in interest and intrigue. By being selective in this way, it is hoped that the insights given can be related to the sights seen on, or near, the walks.

It seems to be widely agreed that the first people to settle in the area were the Neolithic, or New Stone Age folk, around 2,500BC. They would have been the first to have started the process of clearing the forests that once clad these slopes, to make way for crops and grazing. Their settlements would have been made of timber, of which nothing now remains. They did, however, bury their dead in large communal tombs, or cromlechau, of which one of the best concentrations is in and around the Rhiangoll Valley. A particularly good example can be found at Gwern-vale (OS 212192), about half a mile (0.8 kilometre) to the north-west of Crickhowell, just off the A40. These burial chambers seem to be found in areas where there are light soils so it was probably only necessary to clear away light scrub woodland rather than established forest areas, in order to construct their tombs. Gwern-vale, which can be viewed from the road, seems to have been a long cairn housing four chambers. (Incidentally, nearby Gwern-vale Manor, although from rather more recent times, was the birthplace, in 1790, of Sir George Everest, a previous Ordnance Surveyor General of India, and after whom Mount Everest was named). A further example of a cromlech can be found near the farm of Ty Isaf, or Tyisha (OS 183289), to the south of Castell Dinas at the head of the Rhiangoll Valley, and is passed on the walk traversing Mynydd Troed and Mynydd Llan-gorse ('Troed and Tested').

From around 1,700BC people started to gradually migrate into the area from the continent, including those who became known as the *Beaker Folk*, so named because of their habit of burying small pottery beakers in their graves. With them they brought new skills in tool and metal making. These Bronze Age people were the first to use metal instruments in the form of bronze alloys (a mixture of copper and tin) to both clear and cultivate the land. They were also more prolific in their erection of stone structures. Probably the best example of a standing stone from this period is Maen Llia, set in the western Fforest Fawr. There is, luckily, another good example at Maen Llwyd (OS 228277), more locally positioned on the south-western slopes of Pen y Gadair Fawr. How and why these stones were erected is one of the mysteries of this period which still await further exploration and investigation.

The use of bronze eventually evolved into the use of iron and with this evolution, around 500BC, dawned the Iron Age, although its influence didn't reach our area until around 250BC. It was during the Iron Age that the construction of the hilltop fortifications occurred, remains of which can still be found on the higher elevations of the Park. Two of the best examples in the Black Mountains are to be found at Castell Dinas (OS 179301), overlooking the Rhiangoll and Llynfi Valleys, and Crug Hywel (OS 226207), overlooking Crickhowell (and from which, incidentally, the town gets its name). It is all too easy to sit at these spots and conjure up all sorts of wild and romantic images of Iron Age warriors standing guard over the surrounding hills. By way of a bonus, these two sites are also encountered in our walks.

The next to come (or perhaps more accurately, march) were the Romans as they swept westwards in their bid to conquer and subdue the two wild Welsh tribes of the Silures, led by their leader Caratacus, and the Ordovices. In truth, it was probably the Silures who gave the legionnaires their biggest headache, as they were the first opponents of any substance the invaders had faced after the relatively straightforward conquest of Southern England. The Silures had, in fact, fallen back to South Wales after being defeated by the Romans in south-eastern England in 47AD, but still refused to lie down and be quiet until their final subjugation in 74AD by the Roman governor Julius Frontinus. Whilst there is not a particularly strong preponderence of documentary evidence relating to the occupation in the Black Mountains, the Romans would have doubtless been well aware of the strategic importance of the area as a potential stronghold as they beetled back and forth between their fort at Y Gaer (Cicutio), near Brecon and Abergavenny, *en route* for Caerleon (Isca). There was certainly a presence at Abergavenny, as this was the old Roman station of Gobannium, so named after the River Gobannius, or Gafenni as we now know it.

Dark times followed the tactical withdrawal of the Roman Empire at around 400AD. The occasional beam of light would have been held aloft by Celtic missionaries, as, with the zeal and energy for which they became known, they tried to tame the less ruly elements. St. Paulinus, tutor to St. David, patron saint of Wales, established a religious community on the shores of Llangorse Lake (Llyn Syfaddan) during the 6th century. Llanthony, the location of a 12th century Augustinian Priory, was originally a site of some considerable religious significance, the small chapel originally founded here was dedicated to, and quite probably built by, St. David himself. The National Park as a whole has a number of religious sites dedicated to these 5th and 6th century apostles; St. Catwg at Llangatwg (Llangattock); St. Cynidr at Llangynidr; St. Brynach at Llanfrynach and St. Teilo at Llandeilo; and this is almost certainly not exhaustive.

Next on the stage were the Normans who overcame the area with their typical authoritative stamp, manifesting itself firstly in the form of wooden, and then stone, fortifications. By 1088 the invasion of King William 1st had reached the Welsh borderlands and moved up the Wye Valley under the command of Bernard Newmarch (de Neufmarche), King William's half brother. Initially he set up strongholds, known as motte and bailey fortifications. Compared with the sophistication of later castle design, these were relatively crude affairs, albeit eminently functional, consisting of mounds of earth and rubble topped with a ring of wooden palisades alongside an earthwork enclosure. Then, as the grip of the Conquest slowly tightened (and, all credit due to the locals, it **was** slow), these structures were replaced by stone castles of much more strength and substance. They were thoughtfully positioned, too, at strategic points to guard valleys and passes, and thus secured and controlled marching routes and lines of communication. One such site, already well exploited by the Iron Age warriors and mentioned earlier, was Castell Dinas, south of Talgarth. Some people maintain that this is the highest site of any castle in

Wales and England. Other Norman castle remains can be found at Hay-on-Wye, the point at which the Norman invaders first entered Wales, Tretower, Crickhowell, Abergavenny and Bronllys, the last two falling just outside the National Park boundary.

By virtue of his conquest of the Princedom of Brycheiniog, Bernard Newmarch set himself up as the first Marcher Lord of Brecon. This really made him the big cheese, standing largely independent of the King. By and large, the Welsh and their Norman overlords lived fairly harmoniously, cheek by jowl, albeit that there was the odd flare up from time to time. The woodland clearances continued up the valleys giving, more or less, the landscape we enjoy today; the valleys were taken over by agriculture and the wild upper moorlands given over to sheep grazing.

Industry did not make a particularly significant impact on the landscape of the Black Mountains but there is, here and there, evidence of mining, quarrying and iron smelting. Most of these activities seemed to centre around Clydach and the south of the area rather than the 'hills and valleys' of the Black Mountains. This is probably of no surprise given the presence, hereabouts, of both iron ore and limestone. This, together with an enormous supply of wood and the surging power of Afon Clydach as it crashed its way down through the steep rocky gorge, all came together as if by some form of divine intervention. Nowadays the Cwm Clydach Nature Reserve preserves for all our benefits the beautiful native beech woods that clothe the slopes of the gorge. It is possible to visit the old iron works, built some 200 years before the Industrial Revolution really got underway. Iron forges were also sited at Glangrwyne, near the point where Afonydd Grwyne and Usk (Wysg) converge, just north of Gilwern; and at Garnddyrys, on the slopes of the Blorenge, near Abergavenny. The forge here was sited at a surprising altitude, near the 1,300 feet contour. The reasoning behind this was that the site was conveniently near the Brecon and Abergavenny canal, and quite close to the wharf on the canal at Llan-ffwyst (Llanfoist). The forge only operated for about 40 years, and was upstaged by the arrival of the railway at Blaenafon in 1860. It was remarkably productive during its short lifespan, and records show that the forge produced around 300 tons of finished wrought iron products each week.

There was also fairly extensive quarrying activity up and around the Llàngatwg escarpment but, by complete contrast to its past, part of this is now the site of a National Nature Reserve and home to a vast complex of caves, including the famous Agen Allwedd system.

It would be unforgivable to cover, even briefly, the history of the Black Mountains without giving due attention to either Llanthony (Llanddewi Nant Hodni) or Capel-y-ffin, both situated in the Vale of Ewyas. Llanthony Priory is variously written about as being both a priory and an abbey, but, strictly speaking, Llanthony Abbey was the abbey at Capel-y-ffin which was built by Father Ignatius (see later reference). Llanthony Priory was founded around 1100 by William de Lacy, brother of Hugh de Lacy (Lord of Ewyas Lacy), as an Augustinian priory. Inspired by the example set earlier by St. David when he put up a small cell here, William 'renounced the world and its pleasures, repaired the cell of St. David in such a manner as to make it habitable and there dwelt, giving himself up to contemplation and prayer'. The word of the hermit knight's renunciation of the sins of the world reached the ears of Queen Maud, the wife of Henry I. Ernisius (or Ernesius), the Queen's chaplain resolved to team up with William in his pious venture, and joined him as a partner and companion in the newly restored cell. There was, as mentioned earlier, a religious settlement here prior to this, the original site of Llanddewi Nant Hodni, credited as being built by St. David himself in the 6th century, in the form of a mud and wattle monastic cell. It is said to have been 'a poor building, covered with moss and ivy and surrounded with thickets, scarcely habitable for man or beast'.

William therefore could not legitimately claim a 'first' here! William and Ernisius slowly replaced the cell with a church which, in 1108, was consecrated and dedicated to St. John the Baptist, the patron saint of hermits. Hugh de Lacy offered wealth and land to his kinsman which, at first, William turned down. Finally, and with the sanction of Anselm, Archbishop of Canterbury, the offer was accepted and the Priory, the ruins of which we see today, was built. The completion of the Priory is believed to have been around 1120, only some 50 years after the Norman invasion.

Further up the Vale of Ewyas is the delightful hamlet of Capel-y-ffin. Here are to be found two small and secluded chapels as well as the remains of the monastery that became known as Llanthony Tertia (there already being a Llanthony and Llanthony Secunda). In 1870, the Rev. Joseph Lester Lyne set about building his own abbey, or monastery, having unsuccessfully tried to buy Llanthony Priory. He named himself Father Ignatius, somewhat to the suspicion of local folk, and succeeded in attracting a number of followers. However, the fates conspired against him, chiefly from the point of view of Capel-y-ffin's inaccessibility, and the 'Father's' prolonged absences on preaching tours. He died in Surrey in 1908 but was brought back to his monastery to be buried. His grave can be seen in the ruins of the abbey, surrounded by railings. The following slowly started to break up and the site became derelict. Then, in 1924, it was bought by the artist and sculptor Eric Gill, whose aim was to establish an artistic circle there. He, too, gave up the venture, (due in large part to the fact that his sculptures were constantly being damaged during the bumpy cart ride down the valley) and he left the site in 1928, only to return for short visits.

The Landscape

The geological structure of the Black Mountains is basically made up of Devonian, or *old red sandstone*, with only one limestone outcrop around the heights of Pen Cerrig Calch (*calch* being the Welsh for limestone). In fact, in this respect, Pen Cerrig Calch is unique within the whole of the National Park in being the only limestone summit in an area that is otherwise completely dominated by sandstone. It is believed that this red sandstone layer is one of the thickest and most significant in Wales and England, estimated as ranging between 8,000 and 10,000 feet (2,400 to 3,000 metres) thick. The sandstone was deposited here by large meandering rivers flowing slowly over huge tracts of floodplain during what geologists call the Devonian period, about 350 to 390 million years ago. This is brought into perspective when considering that this was a period spanning 40 million years!

Although generically referred to as *old red sandstone*, its colours varied somewhat across the Park, covering brown, red and purple hues, interbedded with red marls. It is the *red marl* that makes up the rock under the foothills of the Black Mountains. *Red marl* is, in fact, a sub-division of the Devonian period. The hills themselves, however, are made up of two of the hardest and most erosion resistant of the Devonian rocks; *brownstones* and *conglomerates*. Over the years the *brownstones* have weathered to the rounded hills with which we are familiar (or are soon about to be). The *brownstones* were gradually built up, layer on layer, to form a band around 1,500 feet (460 metres) thick, interbedded with *red marls* and *conglomerates*. It is this layering effect, together with the resistance of these rocks, that gives us the very characteristic table top appearance of some of these mountains, especially when viewed from the north, where the flat tops give way to the steep northern escarpments. These tough *sandstones* and *conglomerates* come together to form hard bands of rock known as *plateau beds*, seen to best effect in the Black Mountains in summits such as Waun Fach, Pen y Gadair Fawr and Pen-allt Mawr, clearly visible from the summit of Mynydd Troed across the Rhiangoll Valley to the west. These *plateau bed* summits display flat tops and steep sides. This effect can also be clearly seen on both Pen y Fan and Corn Du; indeed, the summit of Corn Du, when viewed from Pen y Fan almost looks as if it were lowered by crane onto a smaller base. *Old red sandstone* is a rock which absorbs water, forming a watershed and hosting the source of a large number of streams and rivers. This explains the large number of reservoirs in the Park, although the only one to be found in our patch is Grwyne Fawr.

As is always the case, it is the nature of the rocks that dictate the nature of the soil which, in turn, dictates the nature of the flora and, to a lesser extent, the fauna. Above the thickly wooded/afforested valleys (a combination of mother nature and a substantial dollop of Forest Enterprise, creeping insidiously up the hillside), the Black Mountains are dominated by heath and moorland. For the most part this consists of a grass-heath carpet, giving out to heather, bilberry, cottongrass and bracken further up the slopes. Inevitably what grows here is dictated by sheep grazing, which is fairly intense, and complemented by the high numbers of ponies that also graze in this part of the Park.

The deep layers of peat which underlie this moorland landscape also have a somewhat limiting effect on the diversity of plants that can flourish here, due to the strong acidic nature of the stuff. Look out, however, for the little yellow heads of tormentil and, in the boggier parts of the heath, the purple flowering (and fly consuming) butterwort, with its characteristic star pattern leaf arrangement.

Down in the valleys the vegetation is more lush and of greater variety. Woodlands are mostly populated by alder trees where the ground is marshy (as in Cwm Coedycerrig on the way from Lower Cwmyoy (Cwm-iou) to Grwyne Fawr), and in other places by beech, birch, and oak. It is interesting to note that the ridgeway between the valleys of Ewyas and Grwyne Fawr is known as Ffawyddog (or Ffawddog, or even Ffwddog) Ridge; 'ffawydden' being the Welsh word for beech. Whilst no doubt considerably less common than they once were, they are still present in the Grwyne Fawr valley, near Blaen-y-cwm at the top of the road, and a beautiful beechwood still thrives at Clydach Gorge.

The Walks

As mentioned earlier, the relatively gentle and rolling nature of the terrain prevents walks in the Black Mountains from being too severe. Nowhere is the walking particularly difficult (unless you are singularly unfit or overweight). There are no crags or other rocky excrescences to get caffled up in; in fact the only real opportunities to get hand to rock are up on the Llangatwg escarpment, and, to a lesser extent, on the summit of the Sugar Loaf (Pen-y-fâl). The greatest challenges to your legs will certainly be the ascents up onto, and descents down off, the ridges, but it has to be said that even these are not particularly arduous (with the possible exception of the descent off the northern slope of Skirrid [Ysgyryd] Fawr). And the ridge walking in these parts is what really gives the Black Mountains their well founded reputation as 'leg stretching' country. The 'there and back' default for walking in the Black Mountains is to ascend a ridge, stride out along its length, and descend to return to the start by way of valleys and fields.

All the walks described in this book, with one exception, fall within the area to the east of the Usk Valley (or Ystradwy, as it was once known). The exception is the Llangatwg Escarpment, which is so near Crickhowell that the reader may well have gone and explored it had it been left out. I hope purists can find it in their hearts to turn a blind eye to this minor geographical discrepancy?

By definition any criteria laid down for grading a walk are bound to be subjective. What, for one walker, is a pleasant stroll, could be of Himalayan proportions to another. All sorts of variables creep in to thwart the formulas; I would be hard pressed to walk according to the well publicised Naismith's Formula which fails utterly to allow for stops to capture the scenery (or several deep breaths), take photographs or grab a lunch break. For this reason I have graded the walks in this area more in terms of their ups and downs rather than in terms of their length. By this criterion a long, but relatively ascent and descent free walk would be graded as easy. Entirely arbitrarily, therefore, I have laid down the following guidelines. They are meant to be just that, and hopefully should help you plan when deciding if you are tackling a day walk or an afternoon stroll. As a loose rule of thumb, I normally allow for an average of about 2 miles an hour; that seems to cover ascents, descents and a few stops.

■ relatively few inclines	Easy
■ some uphill collarwork here	Moderate
■ fairly strenuous walk, involving steep ascents/descents	Strenuous

The introduction to each walk indicates the nature of the terrain that you will encounter, and I have not allowed myself to become too hidebound by the above criteria if it doesn't seem sensible to do so.

All distances are quoted in good old imperial measurements but have their metric equivalent bracketed after them – on occasions this does look a little clumsy (call me old fashioned but 'about 100 yards' is somehow strangely meaningful whereas 'about 92 metres' doesn't sound quite right), but nevertheless both are there to act as a guide. Neither measurement should be construed as being absolutely definitive. Where distances have not been quoted, it is intended that the landmarks indicated in the text are so obvious as to render the quoting of them a bit irrelevant. The term 'half left/right' in the walks' directions signifies a 45° turn whereas 'left/right' signifies a 90° turn.

In terms of how to kit up for walking in the Black Mountains, it is vital to bear a few pointers in mind. A significant amount of the walking described is on exposed hillsides offering precious little in the way of shelter, and whilst the highest point reached is 'only' 2,660 feet (811 metres), on Waun Fach, it can be mightily unpleasant when a fog comes down or rain whips in your face. Weather can be very fickle here and this area has a higher than average rainfall; why else did our forefathers see fit to build a reservoir all the way up the top of the Grwyne Fawr valley? In short, be prepared. Bring spare clothing (particularly pullovers and socks), a map, compass, torch and whistle. Know that, if the worst comes to the worst, the emergency distress signal is six blasts on a whistle or flashes on a torch (or loud shouts if necessary), followed by a minute's pause then repeated. The acknowledgement is three blasts/flashes/shouts.

The nature of the land is also such that there are tracts of black, soft and gooey muck on the upper reaches (referred to as peat, by those who know about such things), and no shortage of mud in the valleys, so wrap your feet and legs up in something supportive and as waterproof as possible, gaiters being preferable to carrier bags (my brother-in-law still holds me to account for dragging him, unprepared, through the black soup between Waun Fach and Pen y Gadair Fawr).

In terms of what to carry your gear in, a rucksack of between 20 and 45 litres capacity should be plenty for all your accoutrements and sustenance. In fact a 45 litre sack would probably be enough for two (unless you are planning an 'eatathon'). For the walks in this book anything over about 45 litres capacity, although impressive to lesser mortals, could become burdensome (any such wearer is probably setting off on, or coming to the end of, the Offa's Dyke Path).

All the walks in this guide are covered by the Ordnance Survey maps, Landranger 161 and Outdoor Leisure 13, both covering Abergavenny and the Black Mountains. The purchase of either, or both, is strongly recommended in order to get the most out of the excellent walking to be had in this region. Apart from providing definitive routes and rights of way, the maps can help you work out some extensions, or deviations to the walks described in the book. This could be especially helpful if you decide to opt for the Beacons Bus service referred to earlier, in terms of selecting appropriate drop off and pick up points. Each walk in the book is accompanied by a sketch map but this is really only meant as a guide, and should be treated as such. The map should be your bible. The sketch maps do, however, show the points of interest detailed after each walk, the number of each point corresponding with the text.

It is also important to note that whilst every effort has been made to ensure that the details contained in the walks are as up to date as possible, nothing stands still, not least the countryside. From time to time, gates appear or disappear; stiles are renewed or upgraded; paths are renewed, extended, diverted or even closed altogether. On more than one occasion whilst compiling this guide I have had to revise walk details where a gate suddenly decided to become a stile, or a green lane had been blocked off! Hopefully, such changes in detail should be fairly minor, (I will have picked up on any major changes) and not detract from the enjoyment of the walk. Any difficult or dangerous obstructions, however, should be reported to the Rights of Way team at the Brecon Beacons National Park Authority, who act as custodians of public rights of way on behalf of the local authorities.

The 'Rights of Way' team is based at the Park Authority's Headquarters in Brecon. In brief the work of the team involves the following:-

1. Maintaining and keeping under review the definitive map – this is the legal document relating to rights of way.
2. The team has a duty to sign all rights of way where they meet a metalled road and has the power to install signs and directional waymarks to assist landowners with rights of way on their property and to ensure people using them are on the correct line. This is clearly in evidence in most of our walks; yellow arrows indicating footpaths which are a right of way, white arrows indicating permitted paths and blue indicating bridleways: look out for them.
3. Network maintenance – the team is active in maintaining and, where possible, improving rights of way within the Authority's area.
4. Legal matters – the Authority has legal powers to enforce and protect the public's right to use and enjoy rights of way

and also to undertake diversions and modification orders where deemed necessary by law.

There are many kilometres of permitted footpaths and rights of way within the Black Mountains. The 'Rights of Way' team relies heavily on reports from walkers, riders and other users on conditions, obstructions or general problems encountered. Should you have anything to report, as mentioned earlier, or want further information about these routes or the wider network then please contact the Authority's Regional Information Office on Abergavenny (01873) 853254, open from Easter to October, or the Wardens Head Office at Glamorgan Street, Brecon, telephone number (01874) 624437. Also be aware that a few stretches of walk do not cover public rights of way. I have indicated where this occurs, and provided that sensible steps are taken (no pun intended), I do not foresee any problems. Reassuringly, many local people I met whilst researching the walks were most welcoming of those who chose to come and explore their homeland on foot.

Welsh Place Names

Welsh can be a difficult language to get to grips with for non-Welsh speakers (which, for the record, includes me), but to understand a few words, especially in the context of place names on the map, can add significantly to your enjoyment of a walk, if not for your partner as you spit and growl at them! I have attempted here a list of some of the more common names encountered in the Black Mountains; it is not exhaustive! After that you're on your own.

Pen	head or top
Rhos	moorland
Llan	church, or holy place
Cefn	ridge
Bryn	hill
Cwm	valley
Cil	narrow

Mynydd	hill or mountain
Hen	old
Llys	court
Maen	rock or stone
Pwll	pool
Du	black
Gwern	marshland
Ffrwd	stream
Waun	pasture or moorland
Calch	limestone
Llysiau	vegetables or herbs
Nant	stream (and by association, the valley of)
Crug	hillock, cairn
Mawr(Fawr)	great or big
Ffordd	way or road
Tal	end
Garth	hill or enclosure
Fach(fechan)	little
Allt	height or hill or slope
Capel	chapel
Ffin	border or boundary
Pont	bridge

Do not make the mistake of trying to locate the village of Llwybr Cyhoeddus, liberally signposted but never found. It is Welsh for public footpath (just look on the other side of the sign if you do not believe me).

Conservation

One last but vitally important point bears emphasising before we set off on our walks. The National Park is an exceptionally beautiful area with increasing pressure to provide leisure and amenities to an ever growing tourist influx. The recent improvements in the road network, especially recent additions and improvements to the M4 motorway and access through the South Wales valleys, bring the Park so much closer to many more people than ever before. There are certain things that we walkers, as a constituent part of this tourist demand, can do to help preserve the Park for both our own and our children's enjoyment. Always walk with care and consideration; marching up a hill, ten abreast will do wonders for erosion and the resulting scars will take much longer to heal than they do to create! Be aware of, and considerate towards, your environment. For example, don't ever scramble over walls or leave gates open (unless they were open when you found them). They are there for a reason and if breached or left open can cause untold misery to farmers controlling their stock. I know this is a mantra fixed in the minds of responsible walkers but there are many who still forget or simply don't realise the consequences of their actions. Similarly, don't jettison your rubbish *en route*. There are few sights more ugly, environmentally damaging and completely avoidable than empty drinks cans, bottles and crisp packets just discarded along the paths. They were in your rucksack when full so they can't be that much of a burden to carry back when they're empty! Apart from anything else, they present a real danger to livestock who could so easily choke on thoughtlessly thrown away junk. Remember, above all, that the Black Mountains are there to be enjoyed – but not just by you.

The Country Code

- enjoy the countryside and respect its life and work
- guard against all risk of fire
- keep your dog under control – especially important in this area!
- keep to public paths across farmland
- use gates and stiles to cross fences, hedges and walls
- leave livestock, crops and machinery alone
- take your litter home
- help to keep all water clean
- protect wildlife, plants and trees

- take special care on country roads
- don't make any unnecessary noise

As the old adage eloquently puts it, 'leave nothing but footprints, take nothing but memories' (or photographs, depending on where you may have previously read it!).

A PERAMBULATION TO PARTRISHOW

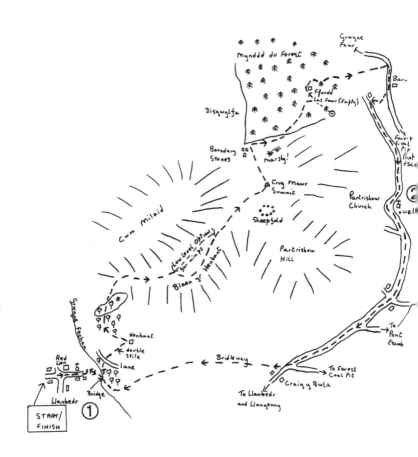

A Perambulation to Partrishow
(Llanbedr - Crug Mawr - Partrishow - Llanbedr)

Access:	The walk starts and ends at the village of Llanbedr, near Crickhowell. Leave Crickhowell on the Llanbedr Road, leading north east out of the town, opposite the old stone wall and gatehouse of Porth Mawr.
Start/Parking:	Llanbedr village, but please park with consideration for those who live there (Grid ref. 239204).
Distance/Grade:	About 10 miles (16 kilometres). Strenuous.
Terrain:	A right old mixed bag, covering tarmac lanes, green lanes, bridleways, and footpaths. The bridleways are prone to muddiness in places. The walk climbs to moorland at around 1,800 feet (548 metres), descends through pine forest and returns along quiet country and green lanes.
Facilities:	There are no facilities *en route*, but the Red Lion in Llanbedr makes a rewarding end to this walk.

The Walk:

Leave Llanbedr (1) by the 'No Through Road' which passes by the church gate. The lane soon becomes narrower and turns into a stony track, doubling back on itself to descend to the Grwyne Fechan river. Cross the Upper Cwm Bridge and turn immediately left to cross a stile into the woods. Do not continue along the track. Follow the path, as it turns first right and then left 10 yards (9 metres) later by the remains of an old tree trunk. Climb quite steeply through woodland. Where the path splits, marked by two yellow waymark arrows, take the left fork and continue uphill. Leave the wood over a stile to enter a field. Continue ahead, up the field, to exit over a stile into a tarmac lane. Cross the lane to enter a second field over a stile, a footpath sign indicating 'Henbant'. Make for the far right corner of the field to leave it, firstly over a stone stile, followed immediately by a wooden stile – a bit like Badminton Horse Trials here! Look for the sign announcing 'Way to Hill'. Continue up the third field aiming slightly to the left of the farm of Henbant Fach. Leave the field through a gate hole and turn right onto a track. Almost immediately, cross a stile and turn left up a steep narrow path through bracken and scrub.

The path crosses a stile to meet a bridleway at right angles. Turn left and follow the bridleway through woodland, to eventually leave it through a gate, onto open moorland. Take the right hand path as it contours the hillside, following a stone wall on your right. The path eventually sweeps round a right hand bend and ascends the lower slopes of Crug Mawr in earnest.

Where the wall finally swings away to the right, the path splits. The main path continues ahead under Blaenyrhenbant, the right hand path ascends the ridge. Take the right hand path and ascend the slopes of Blaenyrhenbant. The path continues along the top of the ridge, to gently descend to the saddle between Blaenyrhenbant and Crug Mawr, eventually rejoining the main path. Continue ahead and, just where the ridge of Crug Mawr starts to climb, look for a narrow path to the right, leaving the main path. Follow the narrow path as it gently climbs to the ridgetop to bring you out just short of the trig point. Turn left along a path, running the ridge, to meet the trig point (OSBM S7275), and grab a well earned breather. There are superb all-round views here, especially the profile of the Sugar Loaf (Pen-y-fâl), resting as it does on its broad supporting shoulders.

From the trig point follow the path north as it descends to the corner of the forest plantation. A section of the forest has recently been stripped away, but the boundary fence is still intact. Near the corner fence post is a set of three rather grand boundary stones, one large one with two smaller siblings either side. They are a little difficult to read but the centre stone displays the narrative 'DINAS Sir J Bailey Bart MP 184 (7?)'. Follow the boundary fence down the hill for about 50 yards (46 metres) and cross a stile on your left onto a forest road. Follow the forest road as far as a sweeping bend to the left, at which point you pick up a waymarked bridleway actually on the bend, leading to the right and downhill. In October the left hand edge of this track plays host to an incredible array of Fly Agaric toadstools, (Amanita muscaria) immediately recognisable by their brilliant red caps adorned with white spots. They are poisonous, the 'muscaria' bit of their latin name means 'a fly', pointing to their former use in a preparation for killing flies. Continue down the track to cross a forest road and rejoin the bridleway on the other side. Follow the bridleway as it continues its descent to meet another bridleway at right angles.

Turn left here and follow the bridleway to the empty farmhouse and outbuildings of Ffordd-las Fawr. Pass through the strangely deserted yard to exit through an old gateway. Follow the bridleway through pine trees to an old gateway, easily identified by a tree on either side. Turn right onto a bridleway here and gently descend. Keep ahead and follow the bridleway as it sweeps round a left hand bend. Do **not** be fooled by a post indicating that the bridleway leaves at the bend to continue ahead downhill – it doesn't! (Perhaps it did once, but now it's blocked off by felled trees lower down). Instead, follow the bend round and, after about 150 yards (137 metres), take a right hand turn (by way of a clue here, keep your eyes glued to the ground for hoof marks). I suspect that this is the bridleway re-routed but it is not signposted as thus on the ground.

Follow the track as it gently descends. Regrettably this is about the worst stretch of the walk, forestry machinery having rendered it into a quagmire, albeit attempts have been made to cover the mud with branches. This makes for very uncomfortable walking, but fortunately it doesn't continue for too long. The track regains some semblance of dignity to leave the forest, exiting onto a tarmac lane. You are now in the Grwyne Fawr valley. Turn right and continue along the lane to pass a barn and yard on your left after about 200 yards (182 metres). About 50 yards (46 metres) past the barn, turn right through a gate onto a rough tarmac drive. (Note that this is not a public right of way, but its use will incur no objections from local farmers provided you stay on the drive and the gates at both ends are secured). Follow the drive uphill to the point where it ends at a tarmac lane, near a barn. Pass through a gate and turn left into the lane, which will lead you unerringly to Partrishow (Patricio) Church (2). Saint Issui's well is in the dip in the lane, past the church, on the left hand side down some flagstones.

Continue along the lane to a junction, about ¾ mile (1.2 kilometre) past the church, having passed two houses on the left. Take the right fork and start to descend fairly steeply. Where the lane levels out it is joined from the left by another lane. Continue ahead to the next junction, a road again coming in from the left. Immediately past this junction turn right between gate posts to enter a green lane (if you pass the house of Craigybwla on your left you have gone too far). Continue along the green lane, which narrows to a path. After about a mile (1.6 kilometres) cross a tarmac lane, and continue ahead along the path. Drop down beside Afon Grwyne Fechan and continue along the path. Do not cross the first footbridge on the left, but continue on to cross the Upper Cwm Bridge crossed earlier at the start of the walk.

Retrace your steps up the stony track to emerge at Llanbedr, and, depending on how you timed the walk, the Red Lion.

Points of Interest:

1. Llanbedr (or Llanbedr Ystrad Yw) is a very pretty and almost sleepy village. It has become, in recent years, a popular starting

point for walks, not only up onto Crug Mawr, (or 'The Great Hillock' – how's that for a term of abuse?) but also onto the Sugar Loaf (Mynydd Pen-y-fâl) and along the lovely Grwyne Fechan valley. The church was originally constructed in the 14th century almost certainly on a site of pagan worship, but was virtually rebuilt, along with the rest of the village, in the 19th century. In reality the tower is the only true substantial part surviving from original 14th century construction, fairly major restoration being carried out by a Mr. Thomas Augustus Davies, in 1897. It was he who presented the church with a brass lectern by way of a 'thank you', when his life was spared from a nasty fall whilst examining the roof timbers in 1892.

2. The idyllically situated medieval church of Partrishow (or Patricio) absolutely cries out to be visited. It was dedicated to a local hermit, Issui, who was cruelly murdered by a traveler to whom he had offered hospitality from his nearby hermitage. A wealthy pilgrim who had been cured of leprosy by the waters of the nearby well, or so it is told, had the church built in memory of the unfortunate Issui. Whilst the church has a number of fascinating features inside, undoubtedly the most stunning is the intricately carved Tudor rood-loft and screen. One of the best examples to be seen today, it fortunately escaped the attention of not only Thomas Cromwell, but also the Puritans **and** the rash of Victorian 'restorers'. Look out, too, for the figure of the Grim Reaper, painted onto the west wall. This has to be one of the most beautiful, and beautifully situated, churches in Wales, if not Great Britain. In spring the church is surrounded by a sea of daffodils, the wild and smaller variety, its approach being artistically framed by the roofed lychgate.

A SAINTLY CIRCUIT

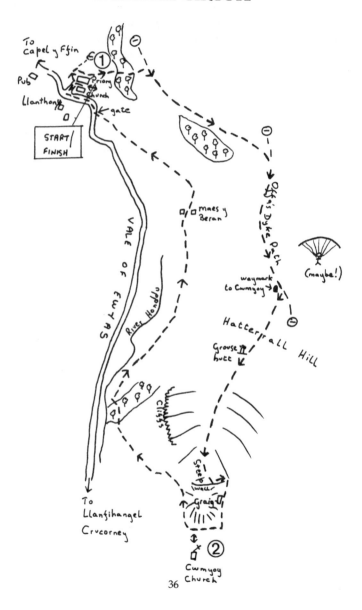

To Capel y Ffin

Pub

Llanthony

Priory
Church

gate

START/
FINISH

VALE OF EWYAS

River Honddu

maes y Beran

Offa's Dyke Path

(maybe!)

waymark to Cwmyoy

Hatterrall Hill

Grouse butt

Cliffs

Steep wall

Graig

To Llanfihangel Crucorney

②

Cumyoy Church

A Saintly Circuit
(Llanthony [Llanddewi Nant Hodni]
- Cwmyoy [Cwm-iou] - Llanthony)

Access:	The walk starts and ends at Llanthony Priory, in the Vale of Ewyas (Dyffryn Euas). Take the B4423 north from Llanfihangel Crucornau up the Vale of Ewyas in the direction of Hay-on-Wye (Y Gelli Gandryll).
Start/Parking:	Car park at Llanthony Priory. Grid ref. 289278.
Distance/Grade:	About 9 miles (14.4 kilometres). Moderate.
Terrain:	Good paths and tracks. Some paths a little indistinct across fields on the home stretch, but keep an eye open for stiles on the opposite sides. The lower reaches of Hatterall Hill are rather steep, just before Cwmyoy Church. After rain the return leg along the valley bottom can be muddy, especially near the farms.
Facilities:	Spoiled for choice here; either the Abbey Hotel, delightfully situated within the ruins of the Priory, or the Half Moon Hotel, about 100 yards (91 metres) further up the valley, towards Capel-y-ffin. There are also public toilets in the Priory car park.

The Walk:

Leave the Priory (1) car park by its entrance, and follow the lane back to the point where it turns left, downhill, to return to the road. The Priory is on your right and the church of St. David on your left. Leave the lane here by continuing ahead over a waymarked stile into a field. Turn right along a track and pass through a gate into a second field. Turn sharp right and follow the sign for 'Longtown', alongside the Priory wall. Cross the stile at the end of the field and turn sharp left, uphill, to follow the edge of the next field. Continue around the edge of the field as far as a stile. Cross the stile onto a broad track which leads gently uphill through woodland. Leave the wood over a stile on your left, and just before a gate, to enter a field. Follow the edge of the field uphill keeping the hedge on your right. At the top of the field cross a stile and turn right onto a clear path, again signposted to Longtown. Follow the path, keeping a rather tumble-down wall on your right. After about 500 yards (455 metres) the path swings left and starts the steady climb to the ridge ahead. Continue up the path until you arrive at the top of the ridge and a junction of paths.

Turn right, onto the Offa's Dyke Path, in the direction signposted 'Cwmyoy'. Follow the wide track southwards as it climbs gently to the summit of Hatterall Hill. There are superb views from up here, both east over Herefordshire and west across the ridges of the Black Mountains. About a mile (1.6 kilometres) after joining the ridge, look for a signpost indicating a path off to the right to Cwmyoy.

The path is narrower than the Offa's Dyke Path and leads off westwards through heather in the direction of Cwmyoy and the Vale of Ewyas. Follow the path for about ¾ mile (1.2 kilometres) past a small stone grouse-butt on the right. About 200 yards (182 metres) past the shelter the path splits. Take the left fork and follow the path down the hillside. Be aware that it gets quite steep in its lower reaches. On arriving at a wall, turn left along a path for a short distance and then swing right onto a stony track (ignore a path over a stile off to the left). Follow the track, which turns into more of a stony lane, a little rough in places, past a rather isolated cottage and garden on your right. About 300 yards (273 metres) beyond the cottage pass a rocky outcrop on the right, known as Y Graig. Immediately past Y Graig, turn left through a gate and descend down a narrow path. The path emerges at a tarmac lane just outside the church of Cwmyoy (Cwm-iou) (2). The church is well worth exploring if you feel so inclined – it is certainly inclined if you are not!

With your back to the church where you emerged into the lane, retrace your steps up the path and through the gate. Turn left along a path and climb gently between two fences. Cross a stream and enter a field through a gate. Continue ahead across the field. Just before a white cottage turn left onto a track. Follow the track to a farm and pass through the farmyard, keeping the house on your right. Enter the field ahead through a gate. Cross the field and make for a stile, about 50 yards (45 metres) up from the bottom far left corner. Cross the stile and turn left downhill to follow a track into a copse. Leave the trees by a stile (ignore the footbridge crossing Afon Honddu on your left) and cross the field keeping to the base of a rough grassy slope on your right. Make for the stile ahead, and from there on to a ruined farmstead. Pass through the derelict farmyard and turn left to cross a stream. Continue ahead across a field, again making for a stile in the opposite hedge. Cross two more fields over stiles to pick up a track leading to Maesyberan Farm. Be aware that the farmyard here can be very muddy!

Keeping the farmhouse on your right pass through the yard and leave by a gate into a field. Turn left along the field, keeping to its left edge. Leave the field by a stile and make for the field ahead. Keeping in the same direction cross four more fields, keeping your eagle eye open for yellow waymarked stiles in the hedges opposite. Finally the path emerges on the road that runs up the Vale of Ewyas (Dyffryn Euas). Cross a stile into the road and turn right. Follow the road for about 100 yards (91 metres) before turning right up the lane that leads back to the Priory and the car park.

Points of Interest:

1. A brief history of Llanthony (Llanddewi Nant Hodni) Priory has already been given in the introduction to the book. The site is exceptionally beautiful and it is only when you force your

mind to erase the presence of the nearby road, do you truly start to get a feeling for just how remote a site it is. Little wonder it was chosen by both Saint David (Dewi Sant) and William de Lacy as a place for peaceful contemplation. I can think of few better places to end a walk than here, with the hills above you and a pint in your hand. The poet Walter Savage Landor thought so too, as he bought the Priory in 1809 with the intention of becoming the local squire. For a short while he lived in what is now the Abbey Hotel, but his short temper and unpleasant outbursts made him a number of enemies hereabouts. He left in 1813, financially worse off after some unsuccessful litigations, his only visible legacy being the trees he planted around the Priory, including some magnificent Spanish chestnuts.

Don't ignore the nearby church, dedicated to St. David, and believed to be on the site of the original cell of St. David. The alignment of the church is such that the altar points to the rising sun on the morning of March 1st; St. David's Day.

2. The little church of Cwmyoy, (or, more correctly, Cwm-iou) dedicated to Saint Martin of Tours, is fascinating for the determination it seems to show for not sliding down the hillside. It is built on one of the south west faces of Hatterall Hill which is cleft with a large landslip, similar in fact, to the slip at Skirrid (Ysgyryd) Fawr. The church, being constructed on the lower slopes of the debris from the landslip, has become contorted as the debris has slowly disintegrated and settled. This contortion is seen to amazing effect from inside the church, looking up the aisle towards the altar and east window. Little wonder that two buttresses have been built on the outside of the structure to support it. I'm told that, of the peal of six bells, only two can be rung because of the alignment of the tower!

The age of the church is not known for sure, but that it dates back to at least the Middle Ages is certain. Look out, too, for the stone cross inside the church, opposite the porch. This is considered to be of some antiquity, a view shared by the individual(s) who stole it in 1967. It was located in an antique dealer's shop in London, from where it was brought home. Note the concrete base into which it is now set! Also of interest are the beautiful memorial stones fastened securely to the walls. A number of these were the creation of the Brute brothers (look out for their initials); the local stonemasons who were particularly adept at monumental masonry, and are particularly ornate – I love the expressions on some of the cherubs' faces!

P.S. There are some excellent postcards on sale at the church!

A SWEET ASCENT

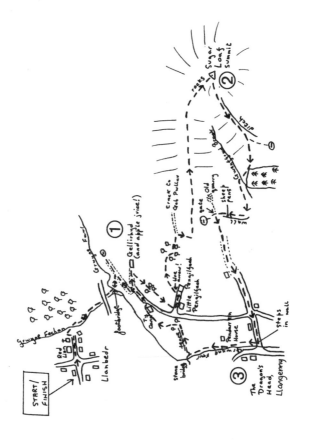

A Sweet Ascent
(Llanbedr - Sugar Loaf - Llangenni - Llanbedr)

Access: The walk starts and ends at the village of Llanbedr, near Crickhowell. Leave Crickhowell on the Llanbedr Road, leading north east out of the town, opposite the old stone wall and gatehouse of Porth Mawr.

Start/Parking: Llanbedr village, but please park with consideration for those who live there. Grid ref. 239204.

Distance/Grade: About 6 miles (9.6 kilometres). Moderate.

Terrain: Farm tracks, green lanes, hill paths, fields and pleasant country lanes. Inevitably there is a bit of a pull up onto the Sugar Loaf (Pen-y-fâl) but this is not particularly arduous. This is a walk for the connoisseur, less busy than many of the more popular routes of ascent. To gain the very best from this walk try it during the first two weeks of November when the 'autumn tints' are stunning, shown to best effect by the beech and larch trees encountered on the way.
Be aware that, in poor visibility, navigation off the hill is not easy – an option under these circumstances would be to retrace your steps.

Facilities: There is the Red Lion at Llanbedr, (advertised as 'The best pub in Llanbedr' – being, in fact, the **only** pub in Llanbedr!) and there is also a pub in Llangenni, the Dragon's Head, about two thirds of the way round. The latter takes in a detour of some

50 yards (45 metres); the Landlord, George, warmly welcoming walkers! Lunches are served from 12-2.30 on Monday to Saturday, and from 12-3.00 on Sunday.

The Walk:

Leave Llanbedr by the 'No Through Road' which passes the church gate. The lane soon becomes narrower and turns into a stony track, doubling back on itself to descend to Afon Grwyne Fechan. Cross the Upper Cwm Bridge and swing right, staying with the track as it follows Afon Grwyne Fechan. Pass a stone footbridge on your right and ascend gently up the track for about 150 yards (136 metres). Leave the track where it bends left, to follow a footpath sign (look for a large beech tree in the junction between track and path). Follow the path to enter a field over a stile to the left of a gate. Cross the field to leave by a stile into a lane. Cross the lane to enter a field, again over a stile. Continue ahead across the field, keeping Afon Grwyne Fechan on your right. Leave the field over a stile and immediately cross a wooden footbridge over Afon Grwyne Fawr (the 'Fawr' and the 'Fechan' join just downstream from this footbridge). Take all sorts of care here – the slats are very slippery after rain (believe me, I know!). Turn left up a grassy track and follow it to emerge at a green lane. Cross the stile and turn right up the lane, signposted Llangenni (the left turn leads to Pen-y-bont). Pass through a gate and continue along the lane to join a tarmac lane. Turn left and walk up the signposted track to Gelli-rhyd Farm (1).

Immediately after passing through the farmyard gates turn right over a stile onto a short grassy track, fenced on both sides. Leave by a stile and cross the field ahead, to leave by a stile. Again cross the field to leave by a stile, into a small copse. Turn right and, about 20 yards (18 metres) later turn ½ left up a gently ascending track. Leave the copse by a 'stiled' fence to enter another field. Cross the field, trending left, to leave by a stile into a tarmac lane, immediately before Pengilfach Farm.

Turn left up the lane and continue as far as Pengilfach Farm. Don't pass through the farm gates but turn left along a signposted bridleway (look for the blue painted arrow on the farm wall with the words 'Sugar Loaf' painted alongside).

Follow the bridleway as it first contours between fields and then gently ascends between larches, holly and sycamore trees. Leave the woodland through a gate and follow a bridleway sign to the right. Ascend the bridleway to arrive on open common land. Pass through another gate and begin the ascent of the Sugar Loaf up the obvious green path through the bracken.

From here the only way is up, as the path safely delivers you to the north westerly end of the summit ridge. This is quite rocky and exciting by Brecon Beacons National Park standards, and a mini crest ascent can be made for those who enjoy such things (great fun in a strong wind). Make for the trig point ahead (OSBM S2117) which proclaims that we are now on National Trust land. Rest and enjoy the massive views, facilitated by the isolation and height of the hill.

With your back to the west face of the trig point, leave the summit by making for the path to your right, running off at 2 o'clock. It is wide, with a shallow trench running to its left and displays a prominent fork further down. Where the path splits, take the right fork, and then the right turn at the next junction of paths. Be careful here, the hill is criss-crossed with paths, but your target is the deep valley on your right, dug out by the Gwenffrwd stream. The path turns to descend to the stream alongside a larch plantation. Cross the stream over stones and ascend the path opposite. Climb gently up out of the cwm and follow the path as it contours round the south westerly promontory of Mynydd Pen-y-fâl. Keeping a stone wall, on your left continue ahead to pass some fenced sheep pens, also on your left. Do not take the signposted path to the left here but continue ahead, keeping with the wall. Continue as far as a path descending from a disused quarry up on the right, and turn left, through a wooden gate, onto a bridleway. The gate bears a small plaque with the narrative 'Direct Route to Llangenny' (probably at one time this path was the main access to the quarry).

Continue downhill, following the bridleway, to meet a tarmac lane. Continue ahead down the lane, which will bring you unerringly to Llangenni (3) (as the plaque on the gate promised). About 20 yards (18 metres) before the road bridge which crosses the Grwyne Fawr, turn right, over a stepped wall, to pick up a footpath alongside the river on your left. Follow the footpath as it crosses several stiles, passing Pendarren House up on the right. At a stone footbridge crossing the river, waymark signs direct you clearly up the field, alongside a fence on your left. Where the fence turns sharp left, continue ahead and ½ left, to pick up a wooden post with the waymark arrow directing you to the stile ahead. Cross the stile and turn left, following the direction of the waymark arrow. Take the track which forks right and, on leaving the trees, take the lower path running alongside a fence. Follow the fence ahead and pass through a gate onto a more obvious track. About 100 yards (91 metres) past the gate, trend right to cross over a stile in a fence into a green lane. Follow the lane, through gates, to pass right alongside the empty house and outbuildings of Ty Canol. Follow the path as it sweeps round to the right, in front of an old barn, to emerge over a stile into a tarmac lane.

Turn left into the lane and follow it back to the start of the drive up to Gellirhyd Farm. From this point, simply turn left down the track and retrace your earlier steps to Llanbedr. (Take care to leave the bridleway at the signpost for Llangenni/Pen-y-bont, at which point turn left over the stile to descend to the river and wooden footbridge crossed earlier).

Points of Interest:

1. Gellirhyd Farm is the home of Daphne and Colin Gardiner, a couple who have turned their backs on the cut and thrust of commercial life and have set up a lifestyle supported by sustainable land management. Amongst other products, they

prepare and bottle (and sell to callers) their own delicious apple juice, grown from the many brands of apples in their orchards. Provided that they are not too busy, they are always delighted to talk to passing walkers and are a mine of interesting information on the area. Drop in!

2. The Sugar Loaf rises to an airy 1,955 feet (596 metres), and is made up of old red sandstone. It was presented to the National Trust by the Viscountess Rhondda in 1936, partly in commemoration of the jubilee of King George V. Strictly speaking, the summit is known as Pen-y-fâl; Mynydd Llanwenarth, Rhoelben, Deri and Mynydd Pen-y-fâl making up the rest of the Sugar Loaf. (In fact, Mynydd Pen-y-fâl falls within the county of Powys and is owned by the Duke of Beaufort.) The name 'Sugar Loaf' appears to derive from its appearance, bearing, somewhat imaginatively, a close resemblence to the results of pouring sugar out on to a flat surface. On the route up described here, look out for what appear to be the remains of ancient hut circles containing, in their centre, four stone slabs, forming a clear rectangle. I have no explanation for them, but that they are of some antiquity is not in much doubt. I have located two, just to the left of the path about half way up the climb, from the point of entering the common. Guaranteed to put on a fine aerial display at the summit are the ravens, always found hereabouts.

Llangenni is a delightful little village, with a strategically placed hostelry for those in need. In fact, the name 'The Dragon's Head' is derived from a part of the heraldic shield of the Morgan family of nearby Maes-y-garth. The Morgans claimed descent from Rhys Goch, Lord of Ystradwy prior to the Norman Conquest. The church is dedicated to Saint Cenae, supposedly one of the daughters of the possibly mythical King Brychan of Brycheiniog, although her original chapel, or cell, was located about ¼ mile (400 metres) distant from the location of the church. An ancient Celtic bell was found at this site, which is now under the stewardship of the National Museum of

Wales. Incidentally, it is to Saint Cenae that Keynsham (near Bath) owes its name.

A Visit to the Witch's Pool
(Pengenffordd - Pwll-y-wrach - Pengenffordd)

Access:	The walk starts and ends near Pengenffordd on the A479 between Crickhowell and Talgarth.
Start/Parking:	End of narrow lane near Dinas Farm. Grid ref. 177304. Note, however, that there has been a spate of break-ins here recently. A more secure alternative may be to park at the nearby Castle Inn, about 500 yards (455 metres) to the south of Dinas Farm Lane, although there is a charge. At the time of writing this is £1.00.
Distance/Grade:	About 8 miles (13 kilometres). Moderate.
Terrain:	Country lanes and bridleways. The rights of way are not readily visible across the fields, but carefully observe the directions of waymark arrows on the stiles and follow them to the opposite side of each field. This is a low level route, perhaps best kept for a day when the clag is hanging over the heights. After rain the falls are quite spectacular, but the approach and the viewing bridge can be **very** slippery, so take care.
Facilities:	None *en route*, but the Castle Inn is (disconcertingly) near the start.

The Walk:

From the pull-in at the end of the lane to Dinas Farm take the signposted track uphill and to the right. Turn left where the

A VISIT TO THE WITCH'S POOL

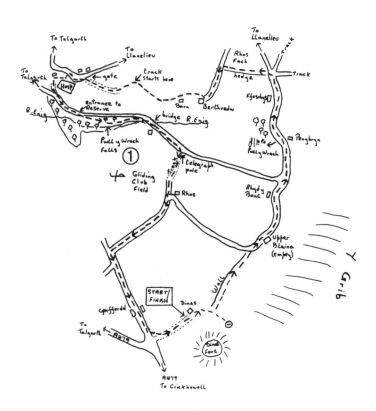

track meets the common at a gate, and with the hill of Castell Dinas on your right. Pick up a rough path running alongside a wall. Do not turn sharp left over the stile here; instead continue ahead, keeping alongside the wall as the path contours the base of Y Grib, to eventually pass through a gate into a country lane.

Keep straight ahead along the lane to pass the deserted farm of Blaenau Uchaf on your right. Continue along the lane for about another 2 miles (3.2 kilometres), ignoring a turning down to the left just after Rhyd-y-bont Farm. Pass a house on the left (Ffos-rhys) then, the length of one field later, turn sharp left along a hedgerow, the edge of Rhos-fach now stretching off to your right. The turn off is readily identifiable, being opposite a bridleway heading up to the escarpment of Y Das.

Continue ahead, along the edge of the common, keeping the hedge on your left. At a lane turn left over a cattle grid, and through a gate bearing the name 'Berth Fedw'. Continue down the lane, and immediately before the farmyard, turn right through a gate into a field. About 20 yards (18 metres) past the gate, cross a stile, left, into another field. Cross this field, aiming to the right, to cross another stile. Keeping to the left edge of this field cross a third stile. Aim in the direction of an old barn and cross a fourth stile, this time keeping the hedge on your right. At the far right hand corner of the field cross a fifth stile. Aim ½ right across the field to a gate in the far corner. Pass through the gate and immediately pass through a second gate on your right. Pick up a track swinging left and downhill, and follow it to a gate. Pass through the gate into an enclosed track which firstly contours, and then turns, right to descend the hillside to a lane by the nearby Mid Wales Hospital (up for sale at the time of writing).

Turn left into the lane and follow it as it swings to the right. Take care not to enter the hospital grounds. Where the lane swings right again, turn left by a newly built stone wall. Almost immediately turn right along a tarmac path to skirt the edge of a cricket field. This is not a public right of way, but it is commonly used by local people. At the end of the path, turn right down the hospital driveway and turn left into a lane. Follow the lane uphill for about 500 yards (455 metres) as far as a large, gnarled oak tree. This marks the start of the walk through the Pwll-y-wrach nature reserve. Leaving the lane at this point, turn right through a swing gate into the reserve. Follow a gravel path leading left through the woods. Where the path ends continue ahead onto a narrower path to the waterfall of Pwll-y-wrach (1). From the falls, continue ahead up a flight of wooden steps and over a stile. Continue alongside the river to finally emerge at a lane near a bridge and a pink (at the time of writing!) cottage. Do not turn right over the bridge, but continue ahead along the lane.

Take the next turning to the right, by a wooden telegraph pole, to walk gently uphill, passing a house on your left. Continue ahead along a bridleway to meet a lane by the entrance to a gliding club. Turn left along the lane. Where the lane splits by a converted chapel, take the right fork. Continue along the lane to a junction. Turn left and eventually pass through Genffordd Farm. Do not take the right turn before the farm. When the lane reaches the A479 Crickhowell/Talgarth road, turn left. Continue to the telephone box, where you turn left again to a green lane. At the end of the lane, turn left and return to the start. If you started from the Castle Inn, continue down the road past the phone box, pick up the footpath running alongside the main road and return to the start.

Points of Interest:

1. Pwll-y-wrach, which means the Witch's Pool, is a Site of Special Scientific Interest and is owned and managed by the Brecknock Wildlife Trust. What the association is with witches is not clear, unless they simply fell for this beautiful spot. The falls are on Afon Enig, which tumbles off the edge of the Black Mountains below Mynydd Bychan. They occur at a point where an outcrop of hard rock (limestone concretion) occurs in the old red sandstone, and fall as a pair of separate, but equally

dramatic curtains of water. The nature reserve, passed through *en route*, is home to a notably wide variety of plants, including wild orchids, dog mercury, wild strawberries and a profusion of bluebells in the spring. Nearer the falls there is a fine collection of ferns and mosses, as well as liverworts.

AROUND THE GRWYNE FECHAN

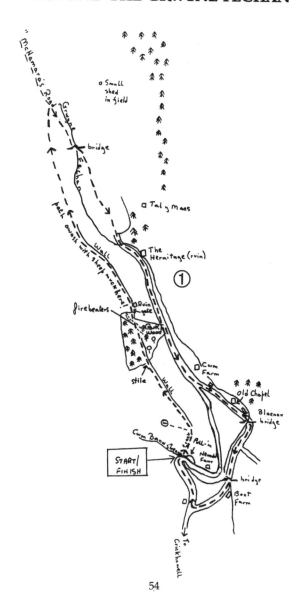

Around Grwyne Fechan
(Cwm Banw - Grwyne Fechan - Cwm Banw)

Access:	The walk starts and ends near Neuadd Fawr Farm, Llanbedr, at a bridge crossing the stream in Cwm Banw.
Start/Parking:	Parking space near bridge. Grid ref. 234229. Follow the lane to Llanbedr out of Crickhowell. At the Llanbedr turn-off (right) continue ahead. Where the road splits at a white cottage, continue ahead and cross the little stone bridge spanning the stream in Cwm Banw. There is space for 5 or 6 cars immediately past the bridge.
Distance/Grade:	About 4 miles (7 kilometres). Easy
Terrain:	Mostly good paths and bridleways. The stretch passing through Park Wood is muddy, and one or two of the trees might have been brought down by recent bad weather. It is quite easy to circumvent these, however.
	This walk is an absolute treat on a sunny autumn day, the remote wooded valley really showing off its beauty to full advantage. The first half of this walk is shared with 'Moving up to Mynydd Llysiau' (walk 11).
Facilities:	None en route.

The Walk:

From the parking space, walk towards the bridge and turn right over a way-marked stile. Follow the sign uphill to leave the field over a stile. Join a stony track, and then ascend gently up the track to a junction of gates. Swing right, staying with the track (look out here for signs stating 'To the Hill' and 'To the Mountain' – and enter into a major debate with your partner about which is correct!).

Where the track passes through a gate into a field, trend to your right and continue ahead, a stone wall on your right. The path (in fact, a bridleway) is not obvious here. Look over the wall for stunning views up the full length of the Grwyne Fechan valley. At the end of the field, cross over a stile into a plantation (Park Wood) and follow the bridleway ahead, still keeping the stone wall on your immediate right. This section can be quite muddy. After a while the wall is replaced by a fence, and then by forestry. Where the bridleway joins up with a well defined forest track coming in from the right, with a row of fire beaters on your left, cross the track to continue along the bridleway in the direction of the blue waymark arrow. Don't be tempted to turn left along the track. Follow the bridleway to leave the plantation by a wooden gate, erected by 'The King's Own Border' (a misprint for Borderers?) as part of 'Exercise Dipper' on behalf of the National Park Authority.

Continue ahead along the bridleway; the open lower slopes of Taltrwynau up to your left, and fields down to your right. Cross two stiles and follow the bridleway as it contours the slopes. About a mile (1.6 kilometres) out of the plantation a bridleway comes up from the right (Macnamara's Road (1)). The spot where the bridleways join is almost opposite a small shed on the far side of the valley, at a junction of fences, in the fields below a large plantation (Twyn-du Forest). Turn right and descend the 'road', crossing Afon Grwyne Fechan over a small stone bridge. (A little before you reach the bridge there is a delightful picnic spot, downstream from a small waterfall – just a thought!)

Having crossed the bridge, ascend the bridleway to the right as it climbs gently across a field to make its way back down the valley. At the point where it meets the gateway to Tal-y-maes

Farm, with a plantation on the left, the bridleway gives way to tarmac. Continue down the tarmac lane to the stone bridge, crossing the river, just before the Hermitage, on the left. Continue along the lane, passing through a gate, to meet a junction, just after Cwm Farm down on the left. From here, it is possible to return directly to the start by continuing ahead, but the more rewarding (if a little longer) option is to take the left fork, signposted as being unsuitable for heavy vehicles, down to the river. The lane, narrow in places, runs alongside the river, passing 'The Old Chapel Grwynefechan', now used as an outdoor activities centre by King's School, Worcester.

Continue along the lane as it crosses the river again, at Pontyfelin, (the house on your left before the bridge used to be a mill) and stay with it as it swings to the right. At the next junction, keep ahead and recross the river at Bont Farm, where it is joined by the Cwm Banw river, actually under the bridge. Ascend the hill and, at the next junction by a cottage, turn right. Continue down this lane to the start of the walk.

Points of Interest:

1. Macnamara's Road (see also Points of Interest for 'Moving up to Mynydd Llysiau') leads to the Hermitage, deep in the Grwyne Fechan valley. It is said that the house was built to accommodate one of the philandering squire Macnamara's mistresses. Judging by the size of the ruins, the original house must have been of some considerable size. It was also built in a rather remote location and can't have been much fun for the aforementioned mistress if the weather was 'in' and the squire was out!

AROUND THE LANDSLIP

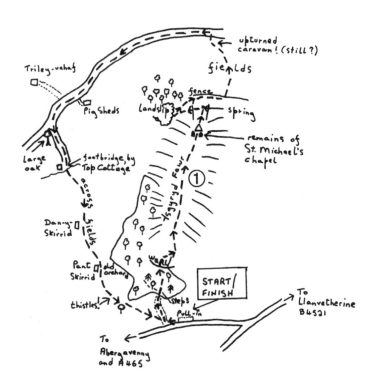

upturned caravan! (still?)

fie^lds

Triley-uchaf

Pig Sheds

Landslip

fence

spring

remains of St. Michael's chapel

Large oak

footbridge, by Top Cottage

across fields

Four fields

①

Dan-y-Skirrid

Pant Skirrid

old orchard

Wall

thistles!

Steps

Pull-In

START/FINISH

To Llanvetherine B4521

To Abergavenny and A465

Around the Landslip
(Skirrid Fawr Ysgyryd Fawr)

Access:	The walk starts and ends near Abergavenny, to the south of Ysgyryd (Skirrid) Fawr, at a pull-in off the B4521, between Abergavenny and Llanwytherin (Llanvetherine).
Start/Parking:	Pull-in, with enough room for about 10 cars. Grid ref. 328164.
Distance/Grade:	About 5 miles (8 kilometres). Moderate.
Terrain:	Quiet lanes, stony tracks, hill paths and fields. The path off the Skirrid to the north is very steep.
	Navigation through the fields on the return journey sounds complicated, but only really demands a keen eye to spot entry and exit stiles, most of which are marked with the Brecon Beacons National Park yellow waymark arrow. It's easier than it reads – honestly!
Facilities:	None *en route*, but there are some rather nice pubs in the vicinity. Try the Skirrid Inn at nearby Llanfihangel Crucornau for lunch.

The Walk:

Pass around the obvious barrier next to the pull-in, and onto a track. Look for a post signed 'Skirrid Fawr 2.4Km'. Follow the track as it first parallels with the road, and then bends round to the right and slightly uphill towards Caer Wood. Enter the woods over a stile, waymarked with a yellow arrow, just to the left of two gates. Continue along the track until it splits after about 20 yards (18 metres). Take the right hand path up a series of steps (again waymarked) and continue to climb to a gate in a very mossy stone wall. Pass through the gate and follow the path, right, as it continues to wind its way uphill through the wood. The National Trust have laid stone slabs to help minimise erosion near the point where the path leaves the wood for more open ground. When the path finally emerges from the wood and into the open turn right along a narrow muddy path, which soon swings left, and opt to ascend either the crest of the ridge, or a little below it to the right. Either way will take you on to the ridge, but the stunning views all around can be obtained that little bit earlier if the crest is taken, and it's not difficult.

Follow the ridge along a clear path, with the panorama continuing to open up, as you make your way up to the solidly built stone trig point that marks the summit of Ysgyryd Fawr (1), at 1,596 feet (487 metres). The trig point bears the emblem of the National Trust who own the mountain's upper reaches, and appears to be guarded by two entrance stones, both bearing strange carvings. Descend very steeply off the north slope of the mountain (you may as well slide down on your bottom – it is quicker and safer, and probably how you'll end up anyway) to meet a path at right angles, just to the left of two springs.

(**Detour** – by turning left here, it is possible to visit the cleft made by the landslip at close quarters – See Points of Interest. At the cleft, make for the bottom of the dip between the mountain and its breakaway over some rocks, and pick up a path leading back in the direction you have just come from. The path will lead you back to the point you would have arrived at by continuing downhill from the springs. The trip is well worth it for the scenery and the solitude this lovely spot affords).

Continue down the hillside, passing the springs and following the stream that flows from them, to meet a second path at right angles. Turn right, and follow the path to the junction of fences on your left. Turn left through a waymarked gate into a field, and continue ahead, keeping the fence/tree hedge on your left. At the bottom of the field cross over a stile into another field. Again continue ahead, keeping the fence and tree line to your left. At the bottom of this second field turn left through an open gateway (the stile here probably feels less than adequate), and follow a narrow sheeptrack. Cross a third field and again leave it by a stile. Turn ½ right across an overgrown paddock, with an old barn on your left, and leave it to enter another field over a stile. Continue ahead through this fourth field to cross a stile, by a footpath sign to Skirrid Fawr, into a lane. (The last time I was here, the stile was hidden behind an old van and overturned caravan!).

Turn left into the lane and follow it for about 1 mile (1.6 kilometres) to a point where it splits, passing, *en route*, a large pig farm (Trileyuchaf). Take the left fork, signposted 'Private Road Footpath only', and 'Llanddewi, Skirrid 4Km'. At the end of the lane continue ahead to cross part of the drive belonging to Top Cottage. Cross a stile, then a stream over a footbridge, then another stile into a field. Cross the field aiming slightly right of centre, between two large trees. Cross a footbridge and stile, at the end of a tree hedge, to enter a second field. Continue ahead, keeping a hedge on your left, to leave the field through a gate, with a waymark arrow on the right gatepost. Continue ahead and slightly right across the field (third field after Top Cottage). Leave by a stile on the far side of a dry ditch, and cross the next field, keeping a farm on your right. Leave the field by a stile, cross a farm track, and enter another field over a stile. Turn ½ left and leave the field over a stile, by an electricity pole, into another field. Continue ahead, alongside a hedge on the right hand edge of the field, to a stile in the far corner. Cross the stile into an overgrown orchard behind a house. Leave the orchard by a stile, and make for the corner of the next field, ahead and to the right. Continue ahead to enter another field, again over a stile, with a farm on your right. Follow the field anticlockwise around its edge to leave it by a stile into the next field. Cross this field (thick with uncomfortably high thistles in summer) to leave by a stile next to a prominent oak tree. Cross the stile, and make a diagonal line to the left and across the field to arrive back at the track leading from the pull-in, and the start of the walk.

Points of Interest:

1. The whole of the mountain above the hill fence, together with Caer Wood and the green lane leading from the car park, is owned by the National Trust, the area being presented to the Trust by Major J A Herbert, MP, in 1939. More properly named Ysgyryd Fawr, (roughly translated from Welsh as 'The Great Separation') its name derives from the prominent 300 foot landslip on its western slopes, caused when a not insubstantial part of the hillside parted company with the summit following the last Ice Age. Local legend, however, tells, far more colourfully, of the mountain splitting at the moment of the crucifixion, hence its other less often used name of the Holy Mountain. What adds interest to this story is that the name 'Skirrid' is also thought by some to be a corruption of the Welsh word 'cysegredig', meaning holy or sacred. Other learned scholars believe it to be a corruption of 'ysgyren', meaning a splinter.

Yet another, even more fanciful, story tells us of a character by the name of Jack O'Kent (a cleric) who bet the Devil that the Sugar Loaf was higher than the Malvern Hills. When Jack was proved to be right, the Devil, in disgust, tried to raise the level of the Malverns by dumping an apron full of soil on their tops, but over Ysgyryd, his apron string broke and the soil fell out forming the tump at the northern end, known as 'Little Billy'.

The actual summit of Ysgyryd is the site of an Iron Age fort as well as that of an ancient chapel dedicated to St. Michael. The chapel was built on the route of a pilgrimage through Wales, and there is documentary evidence of its use during the 17th century as a gathering site for Catholics during the Reformation. By the early 1800's, however, little remained apart from the doorposts. The only visible signs of the chapel today are the two entrance stones through which you pass to reach the trig point. Why a chapel was built in such an exposed and inaccessible spot would appear to be a mystery (nearer to God, perhaps?) but Christian Chapels were often built on pagan sites, and dedicated to St. Michael.

In March 1942, Ysgyryd was also the site of a plane crash, when a Spitfire came down in heavy clouds. The Spitfire was on a training flight and tragically the pilot was killed instantly. The actual location of the crash is in private woodland, the trees having grown over the spot making it all but impossible to find anyway.

CAVES AND CAIRNS

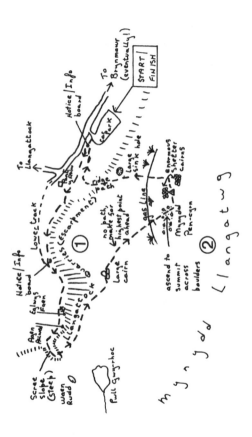

Caves and Cairns
(Mynydd Llangatwg Escarpment and Summit Tŵr Pen-cyrn)

Access:	The walk starts and ends at Llangatwg escarpment, near the village of Llangatwg (or Llangattock), south west of Crickhowell.
Start/Parking:	National Park car park under the western edge of the escarpment . Grid ref 209154.
Distance/Grade:	About 3 miles (4.8 kilometres). Moderate (Easy if the walk is confined to walking along the scarp and returning the same way.)
Terrain:	Clear quarry tracks, narrow paths and some rough and heathery hillside. There is a fairly steep scree slope to ascend, rendering this a walk for the more experienced hillwalkers. In bad weather stick to the tramroads below the escarpment in 'there and back' mode; the mountain top is featureless and navigation is tricky, especially off the top back to the car park.
	It may be an idea to bring a torch on this walk. It is not advisable to enter the caves along the escarpment, but the large cavern of Eglwys Faen is an exception and well worth exploring.
Facilities:	None en route.
Note:	Whilst perhaps not strictly in the Black Mountains, to have missed the opportunity of exploring this fascinating area would not have made a lot of sense.

The Walk:

Walk back towards the car park entrance and look for a National Park information board. From here, pick up a broad grassy path running north and below the escarpment. Follow the path for a few hundred yards and ascend gently to the left to meet some ruined remains of a quarry hut. From the hut continue in the same direction, but along an old tramway. Follow the tramway as it eventually leads between large spoil heaps to the face of the escarpment (1).

At the cliff face, turn right and make your way along its base by following sheep tracks. You can either be adventurous and cling closely to the base of the scarp (and, by so doing, discover some of the more obscure cave entrances), or opt for the tramway a little lower down the slope. Either way, continue ahead to the point where the scarp takes an obvious swing to the left, identified by a National Nature Reserve information board erected by the Countryside Commission for Wales, about the Craig y Cilau reserve. Continue along the track, passing several cave system entrances on your left. These include the caverns of Eglwys Faen, which is reached by a 30 foot (9 metre) zig-zag ascent up to the left, and Agen Allwedd, the entrance to which is protected by a locked steel grille.

Where the track dies away to become a path, continue ahead to an obvious scree run up on your left, the base of which is covered by hawthorn trees. There is no obvious path up the scree but it is perfectly possible to pick a line of ascent through the rocks, by starting to the left at the bottom, and aiming for the top right. About ½ way up, cross the scree to the far side to pick up an ascending sheeptrack which leads to the top, in the form of a hanging valley. The last stretch is a bit of a scramble, but safe if taken with care (notice here a red wooden sign warning of loose rocks – it is far safer to ascend by this route than to descend).

At the top of the scree gully ignore the first track off to the left but opt, instead, for the second. Follow the top of the scarp by a path, which is a little vague in places, and make for a prominent cairn ahead. From the cairn, make a line for the elevated platform to the right, identified by a bouldery incline. Ascend the boulders and make for the summit of Mynydd Llangatwg (2) (the top of which is more properly called Mynydd Pen-cyrn) at 1,735 feet (529 metres) and readily identified by two significant Bronze Age cairns and a trig point (the latter somewhat dwarfed and embarrassed by its nearby, and more substantial, colleagues). There are excellent all round views from here, especially to the east where the skyline is dominated by the high ridges of the Black Mountains, ending with the bulk of the Sugar Loaf.

Descend from the summit in a north easterly direction aiming, on the map, for the edge of the escarpment above Pant-y-rhiw, at GR 205158. Cross a buried gas pipeline just below the summit plateau, marked by a prominent line of marram grass and low concrete posts. You should also pass to the left of a prominent sinkhole about 300 yards (273 metres) after the pipeline. Unfortunately the path, although clearly marked on the map, is not clear on the ground. On approaching the top of the scarp look for a hanging valley to your left and keep just to its right. The footpath descends the scarp, in line with Pant-y-rhiw, down a ridge to arrive back at the tramtrack near the old quarry hut, passed near the start. From here, turn right and make your way back to the car park.

Points of Interest:

1. The escarpment of Llangatwg (more often corrupted to Llangattock) is a natural limestone outcrop, albeit heavily quarried in certain sections, part of which, Craig y Cilau, is designated as a National Nature Reserve. The Reserve is home to a number of rare plants and trees, including species of whitebeam trees. It also provides a start to a number of well known cave systems, including Agen Allwedd, Olygfa Braf (a set of narrow gauge rails still visible at its entrance), Gwalia

Gwynion and Eglwys Faen; systems which are some of the longest and most respected in Britain. Although it is fun to seek out these tiny cave entrances, they should not be attempted unless you are properly 'into caving', and with a person or group who know what they are about. Eglwys Faen is, however, safe to explore, if done so carefully.

The tramway (Bailey's Tramroad) running along the base of the escarpment dates from 1816, and was built to carry quarried limestone around the eastern edge of Mynydd Llangatwg to Bryn-mawr and Nant-y-glo, limestone being used as a flux in the production of iron and steel. In places the stone sleepers, or chairs, which carried the tracks can just be made out.

2. The plateau top of Mynydd Llangatwg is home to a number of sink, or swallow, holes, caused by the collapse of the rock above into caves in the limestone below. Its summit is crowned with two substantial and impressive cairns, possibly constructed during the Iron Age.

Contouring Around Cwm Banw
(Crickhowell - Pen-allt Mawr - Crickhowell)

Access	The walk starts and ends in the town of Crickhowell (Crucywel).
Start/Parking:	Car park in Crickhowell, signposted off the main A40 and opposite the ruins of Crickhowell Castle (Pay and Display). Grid ref. 218184.
Distance/Grade:	About 10 miles (16 kilometres). Strenuous.
Terrain:	Farm tracks, hill paths and pleasant country lanes. There is a fairly steep descent of about 150 feet (45 metres) off the northern slope of Pen-allt Mawr, but it doesn't last for too long. The return leg to Crickhowell unfortunately involves a bit of tarmac trotting, but is pleasant enough and not too bothered by traffic.
Facilities:	None *en route*, but there is a pub in Llanbedr, the Red Lion, should a minor detour necessitate, and there are pubs and tea shops in Crickhowell. Crickhowell Adventure Gear in the town centre, which is passed on the way, has an extensive range of OS maps, as well as some informative leaflets on local walks by local walker and mountain guide Kevin Walker.

The Walk:

From the car park, follow the sign for the fish and chip shop down an alleyway. Turn left and, at the main road running through Crickhowell (1), turn right. Follow the A40 west to just

CONTOURING AROUND CWM BANW

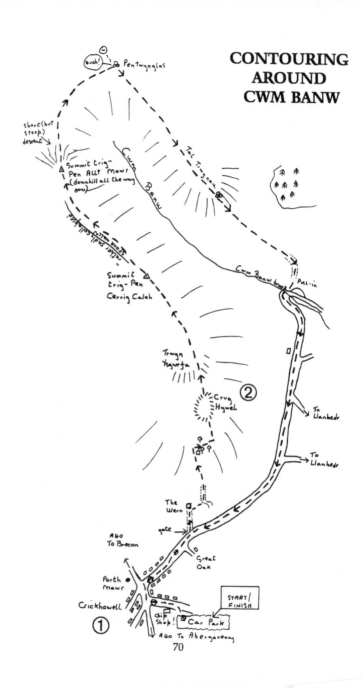

ouch!

Pentwynglas

short (but steep) descent

Summit trig - Pen Allt Mawr
(downhill all the way now)

Cwm Banw

Tal Trwynau

Cwm Banw brook

Pull-in

Summit trig - Pen Cerrig Calch

"old red sandstone"

Trwyn Ysgurfa

Crug Hywel

②

To Llanbedr

To Llanbedr

The Wern

gate

A40 To Brecon

Great Oak

Porth mawr

Crickhowell

①

chip Shop!

START/FINISH

Car Park

A40 To Abergavenny

70

past the stone gateway of Porth Mawr (recently painted cream). Turn right and ascend the lane towards Llanbedr (Llanbedr Road) for about ½ mile (800 metres). Pass through a waymarked gate on your left to Wern Farm. Follow the farm track up to the farmyard and turn right over a stile just in front of the farmhouse. Continue ahead along the left hand edge of a field to another stile. Cross the stile into a green lane and turn left. At the end of the lane cross a stile into a field. Climbing gently, keep to the right hand edge of the field and cross a stile into the next field. Continue ahead to cross a stile at the top of the field. Turn left, and then right over a stile into another field. Walk up the field to a stile in the top right hand corner. Climb over the stile and turn right up a track through woodland, to emerge at another stile. Cross the stile and turn to the left to ascend an obvious green path leading to the summit of Crug Hywel (2). Clear paths lead both up and around the hill.

From the far side of Crug Hywel join the broad path leading directly up the side of Pen Cerrig Calch. The path first crosses the lower summit of Trwyn Ysgwrfa, marked by a large cairn. The summit of Pen Cerrig Calch is obvious, however, being readily identifiable by a trig point and an enormous shelter cairn.

From the trig point continue ahead along a well defined path to the right of a rather sadly collapsed stone wall. The path follows the ridge (generally known as the Allt Mawr Ridge) to culminate at the summit of Pen-allt Mawr, at 2,360 feet (720 metres) the highest point on the ridge, and again identified by a trig point. Descend steeply off Pen-allt Mawr and follow the path as it sweeps round to the right, skirting the head of Cwm Banw. Continue along the path to reach the lower top of Pen Twyn Glas, clearly visible ahead.

On reaching the cairn marking the junction of paths at Pen-twyn Glas, turn to the right. Continue along a clear path, the recently ascended tops of Pen Cerrig Calch and Pen-allt Mawr rising majestically above you to your right. Descend gently down the ridge of Taltrwynau to arrive at a number of disused quarry spoil heaps. At the large and obvious cairn ahead, turn left onto a track and aim for the edge of a coniferous wood. Turn right to cross a stile into a field and continue ahead along clearly defined tractor ruts. The field narrows after about 500 yards (455 metres) and funnels into a track again. Continue down the track, which is both walled and fenced on both sides, to a junction of paths. Do **not** continue along the track which now swings to the left, but turn ½ right over a waymarked stile next to a gate, and into a field. Follow the top of the field for about 20 yards (18 metres) then drop straight down the hill towards a river (marked as Cwm Banw on the map, and a tributary of Afon Grwyne Fechan). Turn left at the bottom of the field and cross a stile into a tarmac lane.

Turn right along the lane, crossing the river over a stone bridge, and follow it for about 2½ miles (4.1 kilometres) back to Crickhowell. The 'there and back' detour to Llanbedr, a left fork about 1¼ miles (2 kilometres) after joining the lane, will add no more than about ½ mile (800 metres) to the journey.

Points of Interest:

1. Crickhowell, an abomination of the Welsh name Crucywel, is a pretty Georgian style market town nestled between the River Usk (Afon Wysg) and the heights of Pen Cerrig Calch. It was once a centre for flannel making when Welsh wool was the prime ingredient, and produced both cheese and gloves. Today, the mainstays of the economy are light industry and agriculture.

There are many features worth exploring, the Bridge End Inn being one of them. But there is also the eye catching (and recently restored) Porth Mawr (Great Gate), on the western exit from the town. The biggest surprise to the visitor may be to learn that there is no grand mansion behind this grand portal, but during the early Tudor period, there was a house here belonging to the Herbert family. There is also the attractive 14th century (albeit heavily restored in 1830) church of Saint Edmund, which was partly built by the splendidly named

Pauncefort family, and in particular Lady Sybil Pauncefort. But possibly the landmark most frequently associated with Crickhowell is its beautiful 13 arch bridge spanning the River Usk (Afon Wysg). It is possible to cross the bridge on foot, there being a series of alcoves to take refuge in, but it still presents a game of chance. I do not know the age of the bridge, although it is certainly of some antiquity. It was rebuilt in 1810, but even despite this, it was considered, by a traveller in 1812 , to present a challenge for the pedestrian. Traffic today is controlled by traffic lights at each end.

2. Crug Hywel after which Crickhowell takes its name, is the prominent, flat topped summit overlooking the town, at 1,481 feet (451 metres). It is capped by an Iron-Age hillfort, Howell's fort, or more correctly, Caer Hywel. The fort was reputedly the frontier fortress of Hywel Dda (Hywel the Good), an enlightened prince of Deheubarth (much of South Wales), Gwynedd and Powys around 930-950AD, whose laws covering what was expected as acceptable social behaviour were centuries ahead of their time. Their fairness and sensibility were never comprehended or equalled by subsequent Norman or English rulers of Wales.

HIKING UP TO HATTERRALL

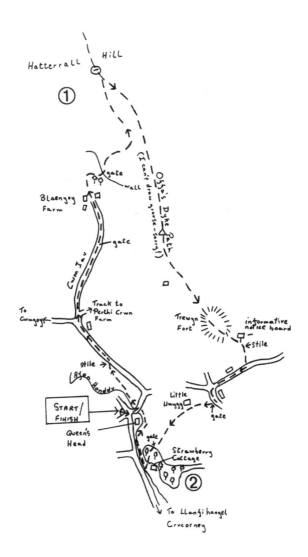

Hiking up to Hatterall
(Stanton - Hatterall Hill - Stanton)

Access:	The walk starts and ends at the Queen's Head Inn, near the hamlet of Stanton, in the Vale of Ewyas (Dyffryn Euas). Take the B4423 north from Llanfihangel Crucornau up the Vale of Ewyas in the direction of Hay on Wye (Y Gelli Gandryll).
Start/Parking:	Walkers car park, opposite the Queen's Head. At the time of writing, the "all day" charge is £1. Grid ref. 311222.
Distance/Grade:	About 6 miles (9.6 kilometres). Moderate to Easy.
Terrain:	Farm tracks, green lanes, hill paths, woodland, fields and pleasant country lanes. There is a bit of a pull up onto Hatterall Hill, but nowhere is this particularly arduous. The fields between the Queen's Head and the lane to Blaenyoy (Blaen-iou) can be muddy.
Facilities:	The Queen's Head serves good food and has a selection of real ales. It is a popular stop for both walkers (boot scraper is provided!) and pony trekkers. The car park is also secure, being easily visible from the pub. The landlord, Mr. Billy Wheeler, reckons there have been no break-ins here for the 32 years he has been landlord!

The Walk:

Leaving the car park, cross the road and take the lane opposite, signposted to Cwmyoy (Cwm-iou). Descend to Afon Honddu, crossed by a stone bridge, and take the signposted footpath left, over a stile, into a field. Keep to the left of the field and leave it over a footbridge. Cross the next field to leave it by a stile and a footbridge (railway sleeper) on the right. Make for the stile diagonally opposite, to the left.

Cross the stile into a tarmac lane and turn left. Continue along the lane for about 500 yards (455 metres) to a lane on the right, marked as a 'No Through Road'. Turn right and follow the lane to Blaenyoy Farm, where it ends. Pass through the farmyard (the dogs are noisy but quite safe) to leave through a gate into a green lane. Ascend the lane, the Cwm-iau stream down on your left, to leave over a stile. Continue ahead along the obvious track as it swings up and round to the right, and passes through a gate onto open land. Stay with the track as it wends its way to the top of the ridge ahead, to meet the Offa's Dyke Path, which runs along the crest of Hatterall Hill (1). (If a little uncertain of the track further up, by making for the top of the ridge you will inevitably meet the Offa's Dyke Path at some point. In so doing, you may well put up a number of grouse too!)

Turn right onto the Offa's Dyke Path and stay with it to meet a trig point (ref. OSBM S6114). Continue along the Path as it descends to the remains of the Iron Age fort of Pen-twyn. Pass the fort's earthen ramparts on your left and continue to descend to a stile. Cross the stile into a green lane and stay with the lane to meet a tarmac lane, still on the Offa's Dyke Path (periodically waymarked with a white acorn symbol). Turn right into the lane and follow it as far as an obvious crossroads. Turn left at the crossroads (where the finger post pointing to the Offa's Dyke Path is on the opposite side of road) to pass a house on your left. About 20 yards (18 metres) past the house, turn right through a gateway marked 'Little Llwygy' (waymarked by a blue arrow). Follow the track down to the house, pass through the gate into the yard, and continue ahead along the track behind the house. At the end of the track pass through a gate and, almost immediately, pass through a second gate slightly to the right, and waymarked with a yellow arrow. Continue ahead along the edge of the field to pass between two gateposts. Continue ahead, following the waymark arrow, pass through a gate, and follow the path as it crosses the field to a gate into Strawberry Cottage Woods (2) (a green notice on the gate informs us that this is run by the Gwent Trust for Nature Conservation).

Follow the path as it descends quite steeply through the woods to meet Strawberry Cottage at the bottom of the valley. Leave the woods by a gate, pass some sheds on your left, and turn right along a narrow gravel path towards a wooden footbridge. Do not cross the footbridge but turn right to follow the edge of the field alongside the river. Cross a stile into a small copse and turn right along a faint path before a stream. The path crosses the stream over a footbridge a little further on. Emerge into a field and continue ahead, keeping to the left edge. Cross a stile and footbridge into the next field and leave it at the far side over a stile on the left, to emerge onto a tarmac lane. Turn left to cross the stone bridge crossed earlier, below the Queen's Head, and return up the hill to the car park.

Points of Interest:

1. Hatterall Hill forms the southern end of the long ridge, starting at Hay Bluff, which defines a fair stretch of the Wales/England border. The highest point of 'The Hill' is 1,743 feet (531 metres), and from the ridge there are superb all round views. On a clear day the Malvern Hills can be picked out, and, on occasions the Shropshire Hills can be seen, profiled against the sky. Enjoy the view, too, down to Abergavenny (Y Fenni) and on to the Severn estuary glinting in the afternoon sun. About 2,700 acres of Hatterall Hill were acquired by the National Park Authority in 1993, the area being rich in archeological interest, including the ancient fort of Tre-wyn, passed on the way down off the hill.

Interestingly, this area is home to the most southerly

indigenous population of red grouse (Lagopus Scoticus) in Britain, the largest breeding population of these 'heather hiders' in the National Park living on the Hill. Possibly some exploded out of the heather just in front of you like clockwork missiles, with their excited, staccato 'clack clack clack' breaking the silence, and frightening you half to death?

2. Strawberry Cottage Wood is a 16 acre nature reserve, now managed by the Gwent Wildlife Trust, and comprising mostly of oak and hazel trees. Buzzards can frequently be spotted flying overhead here, their melancholy mewing often being heard before the birds can be pinpointed. There are also lesser spotted woodpeckers hereabouts so listen out for their mocking call.

Walk 10

Into High Pastures
(Pengenffordd - Waun Fach - Pengenffordd)

Access:	The walk starts and ends near Pengenffordd on the A479 between Crickhowell and Talgarth.
Start/Parking:	End of narrow lane near Dinas Farm. Grid ref. 177304. Note, however, that there has been a spate of vehicle break-ins here recently. A more secure alternative may be to park at the nearby Castle Inn, about 500 yards (455 metres) south of Dinas Farm lane, although there is a charge. At the time of writing this is £1.00.
Distance/Grade:	About 7 miles (11.2 kilometres). Strenuous
Terrain:	Quiet lanes, stony tracks and hill paths. Some of the tracks can become streams after wet weather, so bring appropriate gear to keep dry below knee level.
Facilities:	None *en route*, but the Castle Inn about 500 yards (455 metres) south of the entrance to the Dinas Farm lane could provide an incentive to ensure flagging legs perform the requirements (probably better as a finale than an introduction).

The Walk:

Either walk back from the Castle Inn to the lane to Dinas Farm along the path that runs alongside the road, and turn right to the farm, or from the pull-in at the end of the lane to Dinas Farm, take the signposted track uphill and to the right (depending on your start point). Turn right where the track

INTO HIGH PASTURES

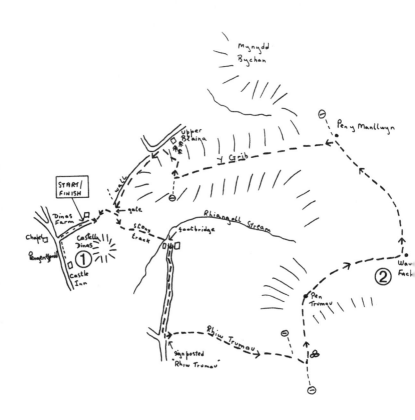

meets the common at a gate, with the hill of Castell Dinas (1) on your right. After about 20 yards (18 metres) join a stony track and descend to a metalled lane. Turn right, crossing the Rhiangoll stream, and pass through a farm. Follow the lane for about ¾ mile (1.2 kilometres) and, at a junction of lanes, keep left. After about 20 yards (18 metres) turn left up a bridleway, clearly signposted to Rhiw Trumau.

Follow the track as it gently rises to emerge on the hillside. Pass through a series of gates forming sheep enclosures. The track continues obliquely up the hillside. At a junction of paths, marked by a cairn, take the path that climbs the broad shoulder of Pen Trumau. Continue the ascent to finally reach the summit of Waun Fach (2). From the singularly undistinguished summit of this lofty bump, head north and follow a path making for the lower top of Penymanllwyn. Make for the ridge going west and leading down to the Rhiangoll Valley. This ridge is Y Grib and is best descended by keeping to the crest until you pick up a broad grassy path slightly to the right. Steadfastly ignore the paths that cross from side to side, and hold your course until, towards the end of the descent, turn right along a wide track. Follow the track to meet a metalled lane near the farm of Blaenau Uchaf. As a guide, make a sort of beeline for a conifer plantation bordering a field behind the farm.

Do not cross over the stile in the fence into the lane. Rather, turn left along the fence to pick up a track that starts at the point where the lane curves off to the right. Continue ahead along the track, keeping a stone wall on your right and the lower slopes of Y Grib on your left. After about ½ mile (800 metres) you will arrive back at the gate encountered earlier in the walk, near Castell Dinas. Follow the stony track downhill to your right and descend to Dinas Farm and the start of the walk. If your start was from the Castle Inn continue down to the main road, and turn left along the footpath to return to the start.

Points of Interest:

1. The hilltop fort of Castell Dinas, right at the head of the Rhiangoll Valley, is reputed to be one of the highest castle sites in Wales and England, at just under 1,500 feet (455 metres). It was originally an Iron Age hill-fort, but was appreciated for its strategic significance by the Normans in the 12th century, who added to it some 1,500 years later. Only scattered remains now bear testimony to what must have been a pretty commanding position.

2. Waun Fach (sometimes spelled Waen Fach), at 2,660 feet (811 metres), is the highest point in the Black Mountains, although to refer to it as a point is stretching things a bit. The name literally means 'little moor', or 'little high pasture', and it is pretty uninspiring despite its lofty bearing; it is best to acknowledge it for its altitude, and then pass swiftly on.

A Walk to the Herb Mountain
(Cwm Banw - Grwyne Fechan - Mynydd Llysiau - Cwm Banw)

Access:	The walk starts and ends near Neuadd Fawr Farm, Llanbedr, at a bridge crossing the stream in Cwm Banw.
Start/Parking:	Parking space near bridge. Grid ref. 234229. Follow the lane to Llanbedr out of Crickhowell. At the Llanbedr turn-off (right) continue ahead. Where the lane splits at a white cottage continue ahead and cross the little stone bridge spanning the stream in Cwm Banw. There is space for 5 or 6 cars immediately past the bridge.
Distance/Grade:	About 7 miles (11 kilometres). Moderate.
Terrain:	Mostly good paths and bridleways. The stretch passing through Park Wood is muddy, and one or two of the trees might have been brought down by bad weather. It is quite easy to circumvent these, however. The upper reaches of Grwyne Fechan are excitingly wild and remote.
	This walk is an absolute treat on a sunny autumn day, the remote wooded valley really showing off its beauty to full advantage.
Facilities:	None *en route*.

The Walk:

From the parking space, walk towards the bridge and turn right over a way-marked stile. Follow the sign up hill to leave the

A WALK TO THE HERB MOUNTAIN

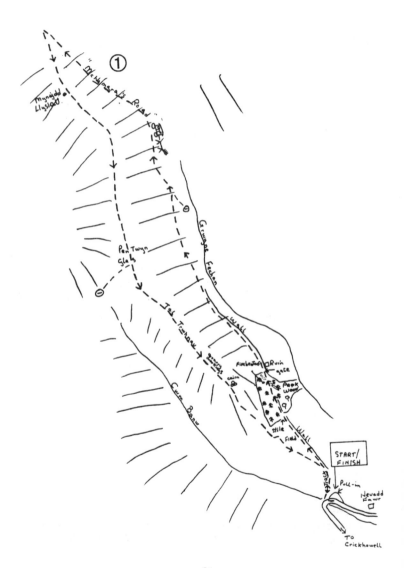

field over a stile. Join a stony track and ascend gently up the track to a junction of gates. Swing right, staying with the track (look out here for signs 'To the Hill' and 'To the Mountain' strategically placed on the bend).

Where the track passes through a gate into a field, trend to your right and continue ahead, a stone wall on your right. The path (in fact, a bridleway) is not obvious on the ground. Look over the wall here for stunning views up the remote and beautiful Grwyne Fechan valley. At the end of the field cross over a stile into a plantation (Park Wood) and follow the bridleway ahead, still keeping the stone wall on your immediate right. This section can be quite muddy. After a while the wall is replaced by a fence, and then by forestry. Where the bridleway joins up with a well defined forest track, a row of fire beaters on your left, cross the track to continue along the bridleway, in the direction of the blue waymark arrow. Don't be tempted to turn left along the track. Follow the bridleway to leave the plantation by a wooden gate, erected by 'The King's Own Border', as part of 'Exercise Dipper' (so the gate tells us).

Continue ahead along the bridleway, the open lower slopes of Taltrwynau up to your left and fields leading down to the Grwyne Fechan river on your right. Cross two stiles and follow the bridleway as it contours the slopes. About a mile (1.6 kilometres) out of the plantation a bridleway comes up from the right (Macnamara's Road [1]). Join the bridleway and continue on to the head of the valley. The bridleway contours below the rocky slopes of Mynydd Llysiau (the mountain of the herbs) and gradually climbs, after a sharp turn to the left, to join the ridge between Mynydd Llysiau and Pentrumau. On cresting the ridge, turn left and follow it back, up a short but steep ascent over Mynydd Llysiau, marked by a small cairn at 2,173 feet (662 metres), to Pen-twyn Glas.

On reaching the cairn marking the junction of paths at Pen-twyn Glas, continue ahead along a clear path with the tops of Pen Cerrig Calch and Pen-allt Mawr rising majestically above you to your right. Descend gently down the ridge of

Taltrwynau to arrive at a number of disused quarry spoil heaps. At the large and obvious cairn ahead, turn left onto a track and aim for the edge of a coniferous wood. Turn right to cross a stile into a field and continue ahead along clearly defined tractor ruts. The field narrows after about 500 yards (455 metres) and funnels into a track again. Continue down the track, which is both walled and fenced on both sides, to a junction of paths. Do **not** continue along the track which now swings to the left, (ascended earlier) but turn ½ right over a waymarked stile next to a gate, and into a field. Follow the top of the field for about 20 yards (18 metres) then drop straight down the hill towards a river (marked as Cwm Banw on the map, and a tributary of Afon Grwyne Fechan). Turn left at the bottom of the field and cross a stile into a tarmac lane. Turn left to return to the start.

Points of Interest:

1. The track which comes up from the Grwyne Fechan valley and which we join to gain the Mynydd Llysiau ridge, was part of an old roadway built by a local squire, a Mr. Macnamara, and is known locally as Macnamara's Road. Boundary stones with his name on are found in several locations in this area (see 'A Perambulation to Partrishow (Walk 1)'). Apparently he was what we might call today 'a bit of a lad', being a founder member of something known as the Hellfire Club. The roadway was built for him so that he could cross the mountain to visit his mistress for whom he had built a residence in the Grwyne Fechan valley, known as The Hermitage – see 'Around the Grwyne Fechan (Walk 5)'. It was to lead to his undoing, however, as he was killed when his coach left the track and rolled down the hillside.

A Hike up to the Highspot
(Capel-y-ffin - Waun Fach - Capel-y-ffin)

Access:	The walk starts and ends at the small hamlet of Capel-y-ffin, in the Vale of Ewyas (Dyffryn Euas). Take the narrow road that leads north up the valley from Llanfihangel Crucornau, through Llanthony (Llanddewi Nant Hodni), or south from Hay-on-Wye (Y Gelli Gandryll), over the Gospel Pass (Bwlchyrefengyl).
Start/Parking:	Capel-y-ffin roadside. **Do** park considerately and **don't** block gates. Grid ref. 255315.
Distance/Grade:	About 9 miles (11.5 kilometres). Strenuous.
Terrain:	Mostly good paths and bridleways. Some lane walking. The section between Waun Fach and Penygadair Fawr is glutinous after wet weather. Take care, too, on the rather steep descent from Penygadair Fawr down to the Grwyne Fawr valley, alongside Nantygadair Fawr (brook).
Facilities:	None *en route*.

The Walk:

From the stream (Nant-bwch) passing through the hamlet of Capel-y-ffin (1), head north up the metalled road for about 300 yards (273 metres). Turn left through a gateway (signed Pen-y-maes) onto a signposted permitted footpath, the access track to Pen-y-maes. Continue along the path as it passes between the buildings of Pen-y-maes and starts to climb the hillside. Join a bridleway coming in from your right and continue ahead. After a short while the bridleway becomes a metalled lane, leading to

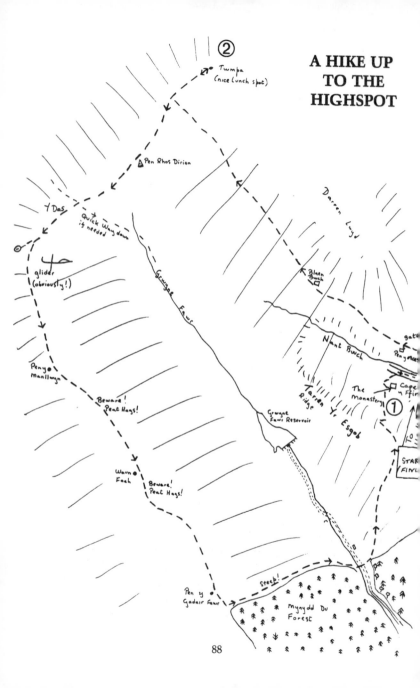

A HIKE UP TO THE HIGHSPOT

② Twmpa (nice lunch spot)

△ Pen Rhos Dirion

Y Das

Quick Way down if needed

⊙ glider (obviously!)

Darren Lwyd

Grwyne Fawr

Blaen Bwch

Nant Bwch

gate

Pen y rhos

Pen y Manllwyn

Beware! Peat Hags!

Tarren yr Esgob

Tarren Ridge

The Monastery

Capel y Ffin

①

Grwyne Fawr Reservoir

TO

START / FINI

Waun Fach

Beware! Peat Hags!

Pen y Gadair Fawr

Steep!

Mynydd Du Forest

Blaen-bwch farm. Pass through two gates at the farm; the lane here returns to being a bridleway. Continue ahead along the bridleway, keeping Nant-bwch below you on your left, until you finally reach the northerly escarpment overlooking the Wye Valley (Dyffryn Gwy). From here turn right to follow the edge of the scarp and gradually ascend to the summit of Twmpa or, perhaps more poetically, Lord Hereford's Knob (2).

Retrace your steps to the point where the bridleway met the escarpment. Continue ahead along a path, the wide vista of the Wye Valley stretching away to your right. The path gently ascends to the summit of Rhosdirion, the top itself known as Pen-Rhosdirion. Continue ahead, dropping down slightly, to meet a track (officially designated a 'Road used as a Public Path') coming up on your left from the Grwyne Fawr valley. Don't turn left down the track (unless a short-cut is the objective), but continue ahead for about 200 yards (182metres), climbing the gently sloping ridge to the top of Penymanllwyn. Below you on the right is the beautiful Rhiangoll Valley, across which can be clearly seen the great hump of Mynydd Troed.

Continue up the incline, the gradient flattening out somewhat after Penymanllwyn has been crossed. From here, continue ahead across a very wet and boggy plateau (we are talking waders here after wet weather!) to the summit of Waun Fach. By way of consolation after the bog trot, you have now arrived at the highest point in the Black Mountains, at 2,660 feet (811metres). With Waun Fach behind you, continue along the broad ridge to the next, and frankly, rather more exciting, summit of Penygadair Fawr, marked by a large and conspicuous cairn. From here make your way down to the corner of the Mynydd Du forest, ahead and to your left.

At the corner of the forest turn left downhill, keeping the forest boundary fence on your right. Take care here; the path is quite steep in places, and can be muddy. On reaching the valley bottom, cross both Afon Grwyne Fawr and the metalled lane (which, if followed left, would lead you to the dam of the Grwyne Fawr reservoir). Start to ascend the lower slopes of

Chwarel y Fan opposite, keeping the forest edge on your right. Cross a bridleway, and turn left onto a path as it emerges from the forest. Follow the path as it ascends the slope at a 45 degree angle to crest the ridge of Chwarel y Fan. The path drops to the left once over the ridge and picks its way easily through the rocks of Tarren yr Esgob. Continue ahead, passing the site of a monastery on your right, to join a metalled lane. Turn right along the lane and return to the start at Capel-y-ffin.

Points of Interest:

1. The hamlet of Capel-y-ffin amply repays an exploratory stroll in its own right. The name is Welsh for 'chapel on the border', situated as it is just inside both the Gwent County and Wales boundary. There are, in fact, two chapels here, the well known whitewashed church near the roadside, and, behind it, across Afon Honddu, a Baptist chapel, both of 18th century origin. The wooden, louvered chimney of the church gives it a sort of squat, owl look. Inside the layout is very simple, with a pulpit dating from 1786, and a gallery, well worth exploring for the bird's eye view down into the building. Look out, too, for the immortal words engraved on the east window 'I shall lift up mine eyes unto the hills'.

The Baptist chapel was built in 1737, and is tucked away under the hillside. From the upper corner of the graveyard there is a fine view of the chapel against the backdrop of the hill of Y Darren Lwyd, rising high over Capel-y-ffin. Quite which chapel is referred to in the name of this solitary hamlet is not clear. There is, strictly speaking, one church and one chapel, so it may well be the Baptist chapel, despite its comparative obscurity when compared to the better known church.

On the western side of the stream are the remains of the monastery of Llanthony Tertia, established by the Reverend Lester Lyne in 1870. A more detailed history (albeit somewhat potted) is outlined in the introduction to the book.

2. Twmpa, or Lord Hereford's Knob, at 2,263 feet (690 metres) offers a superb panoramic view north west across the Wye

Valley (Dyffryn Gwy). The answer to the question why Lord Hereford's Knob (and which Lord Hereford?) has yet to be uncovered.

ON THE BORDER

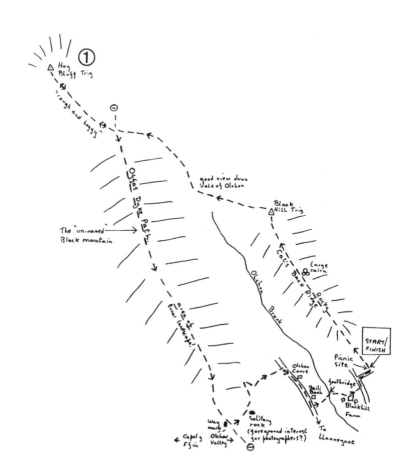

Hay Bluff Trig (1)

"rough and boggy"

Offas Dyke Path

good view down Vale of Olchon

Black Hill Trig

The "un-named Black mountain"

Cat's Back Ridge

Large cairn

Rocky

Offas of Even (undecifer?)

Olchon Brook

START/FINISH

Picnic site

Olchon Court

footbridge

Baili Bach

Black Hill Farm

Way mark
Olchon Valley

Solitary rock (foreground interest for photographers?)

← Capel y Ffin

To Llanveynoe

Walk 13

On The Border
(Llanveynoe - Hay Bluff - Llanveynoe)

Access:	The walk starts and ends near Llanveynoe, beneath the Cat's Back Ridge, a spur leading south off the Black Hill.
Start/Parking:	Black Hill picnic site. Grid ref. 288329.
Distance/Grade:	About 9 miles (14.4 kilometres). Strenuous
Terrain:	Good clear paths, muddy in places after rain, and country lanes.
Facilities:	None *en route*.

The Walk:

From the picnic site, turn left over a stile. Climb a steep path, initially on grass then on rock, to reach the fairly exposed ridge of Crib-y-garth. There is a sort of choice here; the purist can opt for the crest of the ridge proper, or a path just below the ridge may be selected. (The ridge is hardly the stuff of Grib Goch in Eryri (Snowdonia), but if you prefer not to perform acrobatics there is, at least, a Plan B.) Either way, follow your chosen path as it makes its way north-west to the trig point on the Black Hill at 2,101 feet (640 metres), clearly visible ahead and slightly to the right.

From the trig point take the wide path leading ½ left. After about 500 yards (455 metres) the path splits but soon joins up again, so take your pick with confidence. Stay with the path as it contours the hillside, rising ahead and to the left. The head of the Vale of Olchon is now behind you, to the left. About 1½ miles (2.4 kilometres) past the trig point on the Black Hill, the path meets the Offa's Dyke Path at right angles at the foot of a slope on the left. Turn right onto the path and make an obvious bee-line for the trig point on the summit of Hay Bluff (1), about ½ mile (800 metres) ahead. Take care not to follow the Offa's Dyke Path, which veers off to the right about 100 yards (91 metres) after you joined it. From here, there is a terrific view across the wide stretch of the Wye Valley (Dyffryn Gwy) for as far as the eye can see.

With your back to the trig point, retrace your steps along the path, heading south, to rejoin the Offa's Dyke Path. As you will have discovered to your chagrin, this stretch of the path is quite rough and boggy in places. Make two short, sharp ascents to gain the height of the broad top ahead. The top is not named on the OS maps but is locally known as Black Mountain (Grid Ref. 255353). The path continues across Black Mountain in a south-easterly direction, with views of Waun Fach and Pen y Gadair Fawr to the west, and Crib-y-garth (encountered earlier) to the east. As you descend gently from the summit of Black Mountain you will come across a large expanse of bare ground, covered with sun bleached pebbles and rocks that for all the world look like a lunar landscape. Cross the lunar landscape, your way marked by a series of cairns (12 at the last count). Continue along the path until you reach a neat stone signpost at ground level, on your left, indicating Capel-y-ffin to your right and Olchon Valley to your left. As a guide, the signpost is just about level with the road leading up to the picnic site on the other side of the Olchon Valley, where you earlier started.

Turn left, downhill; the initially ill-defined path gradually improving into a more obvious track. The track zigzags down the hillside, offering beautiful views down almost the entire length of the Olchon Valley. At the bottom continue ahead, through a gate, into a field. Keep to the right of the field to pass through a second gate into a lane. Turn right at the lane, to pass both Olchon Court and Beili-bach Farm on your left. Cross a stile about 100 yards (91 metres) past Beili-bach, on the left, into a field. Keeping to the left of the field continue ahead. After about 200 yards (182 metres) the path descends to a footbridge crossing Nant Olchon (brook). Cross the footbridge and ascend, ½ right, up a track. Follow the track as it slowly fades to an obscure path, keeping to the right of the field. The path continues to climb the hillside away from the brook and finally emerges at Black Hill Farm, part hidden in the trees. Keeping the farm on your right, follow the access track up the hill to a lane. Turn left at the lane and, shortly afterwards turn right, up another lane, and back to the start.

Points of Interest:

1. Hay Bluff, at 2,220 feet (677 metres) is the high spot of this walk, and is sometimes referred to as Pen y Beacon. Although not quite as high as its southerly neighbour, the Black Hill, at 2,306 feet (703 metres) the views all around are stunning; north across the expanse of the Wye Valley (Dyffryn Gwy) with its patchwork fields, west across Twmpa and on to the central Beacons, south along the high ridge to the River Severn (Afon Hafren), and east across the agricultural lands of Herefordshire. On a hot summers day there is a perverse pleasure to be gained from sitting on the western edge, watching people toiling up the steep slope from the Gospel Pass (Bwlchyrefengyl), some 700 feet (214 metres) below.

TROED AND TESTED

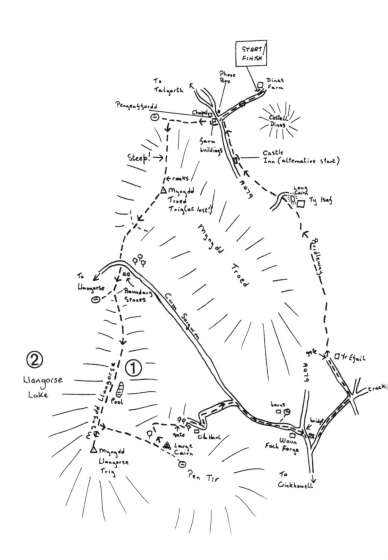

Troed and Tested
(Pengenffordd - Mynydd Troed - Pengenffordd)

Access:	The walk starts and ends near Pengenffordd on the A479 between Crickhowell and Talgarth.
Start/Parking:	End of narrow lane near Dinas Farm. Grid ref. 177304. Note, however, that there has been a spate of break-ins here recently. A more secure alternative may be to park at the nearby Castle Inn, about 500 yards (455 metres) south of the Dinas Farm lane, although there is a charge. At the time of writing this is £1.00, a small price to pay for peace of mind (and the beer is pretty good too)!
Distance/Grade:	About 7 miles (11 kilometres). Moderate.
Terrain:	Mostly good paths and bridleways. Some lane walking. The initial pull up Mynydd Troed is a bit of a grind, and the bridleway back to the start can be muddy. Watch out here, too, for groups of pony trekkers.
Facilities:	None *en route*, but the Castle Inn is temptingly near, and all the more so if you have availed yourself of its car park.

The Walk:

Return up the lane from Dinas Farm to the main road and cross into a green lane. (If leaving from the Castle Inn, continue up the road along a narrow path towards the chapel at the crest, and cross at the lane leading to Dinas Farm). Enter a farmyard through a gate and leave it on the right through two gates, waymarked by a yellow arrow on a green background. Turn left by a row of wooden posts and enter a green lane lined by trees on either side. Stay in the lane to leave it via a gate onto a common. Follow a vague path (mostly sheep track) up to the obvious base of the 'nose' of Mynydd Troed, then begin the slog up to the summit trig point (OSBM S1781), at 1,997 feet (609 metres) teasingly just 3 feet short of the 2,000 foot mark.

From the summit (after an appropriate breather) aim for Mynydd Llan-gors (1) to the south-west, taking the right of the two paths leading from the trig point. On the descent, cross a path and continue down to the tarmac lane coming up from Cwm Sorgwm on the left. Cross the lane (to the right of two boundary stones, one bearing the name Macnamara, 1891) and initially follow the signpost indicating a bridleway to Cathedine. Leave the bridleway and ascend straight up the obvious path ahead, with good views of Cwm Sorgwm down on your left (strictly speaking the ascent by this route is not a proper right of way, but the path is obviously well used by a large number of walkers). Near the top of the ascent switch to a wide path on the right and, where the path divides, take the right fork. Continue ahead along the wide grassy track right to the summit trig point of Mynydd Llan-gors (OSBM S2513), at 1,661 feet (506 metres). Below you to the west is a view of Llyn Syfaddan (2) (Llan-gors Lake).

From here, retrace your steps for about 200 yards (182 metres) to a junction of paths. Turn right and continue along the path to the dip between Mynydd Llan-gors and Pen-tir, marked by a fairly solid cairn. Turn left here, keeping the cairn on your right, to descend a zigzag path down into Cwm Sorgwm. Where the path meets the corner of a fenced field on your right, turn right down to a gate. Pass through the gate onto a track. Follow the track for about 50 yards (45 metres) to a tarmac lane. Turn left down the lane and follow it downhill, then uphill, to join the lane that passes along the length of Cwm Sorgwm. Turn right and follow the lane to Waun Fach forge where it meets the main A479, running along the Rhiangoll Valley.

Turn right along the main road, over a bridge, then turn left 50 yards (45 metres) later onto a marked footpath, through a gate. Pass in front of a house and continue ahead along a green lane. At a tarmac lane turn left, uphill. At an obvious 3 way junction, take the first left hand lane. Continue along the lane to a farm (Yr Efail) and then pass through a gate into a shady green lane. The dogs at the farm are very noisy but pose no hazard (or so the farm owner assures me). Follow the lane as, after about 1½ miles (2.4 kilometres), it takes you back to the Castle Inn, past Ty-isaf Farm, where there are the traces of a cromlech, or long cairn. Just after the farm the track joins a tarmac lane for a few yards then leaves it to continue ahead. If you started from Dinas Farm, follow the track as far as the junction with the lane leading to the farm.

Points of Interest:

1. Mynydd Llan-gors is topped by an extensive plateau of heather and bracken, offering good views across to the more easterly heights of Pen-allt Mawr and Pen Cerrig Calch (a sustained flat top sloping down from left to right). It was, in December 1943, the site of a tragic accident when a training flight resulted in a collision between two aircraft. One made it back to base near Hereford, but the other crashed into the hillside high above Upper Cathedine farm, on the western slopes.

2. Llyn Syfaddan (Llan-gors Lake), at just over 1 mile (1.6 kilometres) long is the largest natural lake in South Wales. It is natural in that it is partially dammed by a glacial moraine of gravel and clay, rather than by the hand of man. It is kept topped up by a constant supply of water from Afon Llynfi. The lake probably owes its origins to the presence of a rock basin scooped out by glacial action, and its depth is attributable to the height of the surrounding glacial moraine deposits combined with the scooped out basin.

The lake is rich in both flora and fauna, and is noted for its variety of bird life. Ornithologists love it here as the surrounding reeds and alder trees provide shelter both for them and those they have come to study; in particular lapwings, coots, shovelers, widgeon and herons.

A particularly interesting aspect of the lake is the remains of an ancient crannog, or artificial island, believed to have been built around the 9th century AD. Typical of a lake with such a feature, there are tales of a buried city here, albeit totally untrue. A village there certainly was, with the remains of a dugout canoe on display at the museum at Brecon. The site has been well explored and has featured in archeology programmes on television.

There is a rather charming tale told by Giraldus Cambrensis (Gerallt Gymro) that Gruffudd ap Rhys (Lord of Brecknock, or more properly, Arglwydd Brycheiniog), Payn FitzJohn (Lord of Ewyas) and Milo Fitzwalter (Earl of Hereford), three local noblemen but only one of Welsh descent, were riding by the lake debating the legend that the local birds would only sing for the rightful ruler of Wales. In true storybook fashion the two Normans, FitzJohn and Fitzwalter, evoked little response from the feathered locals but at Gruffudd's request, not only did they all sing fit to burst, they all but swam several lengths of the lake as well.

Walk 15

The Ridge of Revenge
(Pont Esgob - Bâl Mawr - Pont Esgob)

Access:	The walk starts and ends near the road junction at Pont Esgob, on the minor road between Lower Cwm-yoy (Cwm-iou) (Stanton) and Forest Coal Pit.
Start/Parking:	Pull-in by telephone box, enough room for 4 or 5 cars. Grid ref. 285212.
Distance/Grade:	About 9 miles (14.5 kilometres). Moderate
Terrain:	Country lanes, green lanes, farm track and good hill paths. There is one section where the path is a little vague, descending Bâl Mawr's lower slopes, but it is never really in doubt.
Facilities:	None *en route.*

The Walk:

From the car, walk back to the road junction, and turn left up the lane signposted as a No Through Road. Climb steadily up the hill, first passing on the right the driveway to 'The Pant' farm and, shortly after, 'New Inn' farm on the left. Ignore the concrete driveway on the right, just past 'New Inn' farm but stay on the lane, which becomes a green lane. Follow the green lane as it contours the hillside. Keep an eye out for horses and riders along here – it is a popular route for trekking (look carefully where you place your boots too!). At the end of the track pass through a gate and turn ½ right up a clear track onto open moorland. A stone wall appears on the left. Where the track and wall converge, continue ahead up the hillside to meet a broad grassy track at right angles.

(From here it is a fairly short and obvious stroll to the

THE RIDGE OF REVENGE

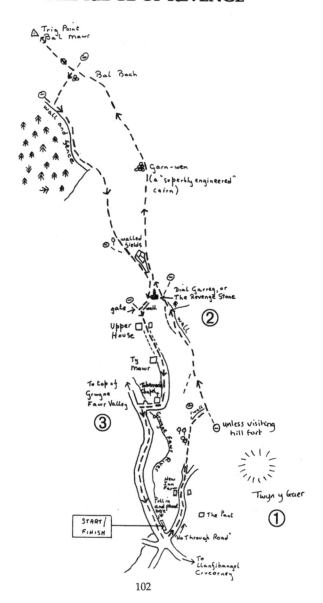

Trig Point
Bal mawr
Bal Bach

wall and fence

Garn-wen
(a "superbly engineered"
cairn)

walled fields

Dial Garreg, or
The Revenge Stone
②

gate → wall

Upper House

Ty mawr

To top of
Grwyne
Fawr Valley

③

Grwyne Fawr

unless visiting
hill fort

New Inn Farm

Poll in
and pool
hole

START/
FINISH

The Pant

'No Through Road'

To
Llanfihangel
Crucorney

Twyn y Gaer
①

summit of 'Gaer' (1), the iron age promontory fort on the right. The extra effort is well rewarded in terms of both views and interest. The prominent hill to the right is the Sugar Loaf [Mynydd Pen-y-fâl].)

Turn left along the track, the views of both the Grwyne Fawr valley (3) on the left and the Vale of Ewyas on the right being particularly good. Keep your eye out for the landslip below Hatterall Hill as well as Cwm-iou church beneath it on the right. After about ½ mile (800 metres) pass through a gate and where the path splits, a short while after, take the right hand path; the split is identified by a solitary pine tree in the corner of a field on the left. (You can go left, but the superb views up the Vale of Ewyas are better enjoyed from the right hand path.) After about 200 yards (182 metres) the two paths join up again at the Dial Garreg (2), an upright stone about 3 feet high and surrounded by boulders to form a small plinth. The stone in fact marks the junction of paths coming up from Ewyas as well as descending to Grwyne Fawr.

Continue along the ridge, following the trackway, and make for the huge cairn ahead, marking the summit of Garn Wen. The track gently climbs out of the rather sheltered stretch after Dial Garreg and onto more open moorland, before depositing you gently at the cairn and 'dugout' shelter. Pass the cairn, built with engineering precision, and continue ahead along the track to the top of Bâl Bach. From here the path is obvious as it descends to a cairn (a good old 'pile of stones' this time). This cairn, like Dial Garreg previously, also marks a junction of paths. It also marks the start of the stony path ascending Bâl Mawr, the summit of which, at 1,990 feet (606 metres) supports both a trig point (OSBM S7281) and an excellent view of the continuation of the ridge as far as Chwarel y Fan, at 2,228 feet (679 metres). If you feel energetic, the continuation on to Chwarel y Fan is a fine extension to the walk. However, you should return to this point for the return leg.

Retrace your steps from the summit of Bâl Mawr down to the 'pile of stones' passed earlier. Turn right onto a path and, about 20 yards (18 metres) later, take the left fork. When the path is seen to split, take the left fork each time. This will bring you safely down to a broad path contouring the hillside above Grwyne Fawr, just above the treeline, and running alongside a stone wall. Turn left onto the path and follow it, firstly along the top of the forest edge, and then across open moorland. The path will eventually lead you back to Dial Garreg. However, about 150 yards (136 metres) before the stone, and 200 yards (182 metres) before the stone wall just past it on the right, take a track leading off ½ right. Follow the track as far as the stone wall. Keep on the track as it hugs the wall, now on your left, as far as a gateway.

Pass through the gateway into a green lane, fenced on both sides. The lane leads down to Upper House. Pass through a gate into the farmyard and, keeping the farmhouse on your right, leave it through a second gate. Descend a tarmac lane through a field to pass the house of Ty Mawr on your right. Look out for peacocks in the garden! Continue down the lane to arrive at Tabernacle Chapel and the Grwyne Fawr river. The chapel graveyard is worth a short visit – there are some beautifully carved and inscribed headstones.

From the chapel, cross the river bridge and turn left down the road which runs the length of the Grwyne Fawr valley, to return to the start.

Points of Interest:

1. Twyn-y-gaer, at 1,399 feet (426 metres) is an Iron Age encampment. It is oval in shape and divided into 3 sections, collectively covering about 4½ acres. The main entrance is approached by a sunken passage and is well protected by a double embankment. Interestingly it is the middle of a line of three such forts, the other two being Crug Hywel to the west; and Tre-wyn to the east, at the southern edge of Hatterall Hill.

2. Dial Garreg is Welsh for the Revenge Stone, and is said to mark the site of an older and larger memorial stone, placed there to identify the spot where the Norman Marcher Lord,

Richard de Clare, was attacked and killed by Morgan ap Owen, and his followers. Morgan was the Welsh Lord of Caerleon and, in 1135, a concerted effort was made by the Welsh to drive the Norman oppressors out of Wales, at a time of turmoil following the death of Henry I. De Clare had been accompanied for part of his journey by Brian de L'isle (or Fitzcount, as he was also known) as far as the mouth of Afon Grwyne Fechan. Quite possibly De Clare felt there was less likelihood of being attacked on an exposed ridge than in the secluded and sheltered valley; if so, it was an error of judgement that cost him his life.

3. It is strange to imagine the Grwyne Fawr valley without a road running along its length, but this was the case until not so long ago. The road was only completed in 1912, and only then as a means of access to the Grwyne Fawr Reservoir 'Works', and the village of Blaen-y-cwm, which was built to house the 'navvy' workforce. Prior to that there had been a track running part way up the valley bottom, which then climbed to continue along the hillside below Bâl Mawr. The road was built under contract for the Abertillery and District Water Board, under whose direction the construction on the reservoir started in 1912 and continued 1928. The final bill for the whole reservoir project, comprising the reservoir, the now non-existent village of Blaen-y-cwm (at the top of the valley, and two miles below the reservoir), the road (also overlaid with a railway line) and a tunnel and pipes from the site to the Nantydraenog reservoir, just outside Crosskeys, came to just over one million pounds, a hefty sum indeed in 1928. At the height of construction, the village of Blaen-y-cwm was home to around 400 workers and their families. Today, little remains to point to the massive efforts to construct such a challenging piece of infrastructure.

Some Useful Addresses

Brecon Beacons National Park Authority, 7 Glamorgan Street, Brecon LD3 7DP. Tel: 01874 624437

National Trust, Dan-y-gyrn, Blaen-glyn Farm, Libanus, Brecon LD3 8NF. Tel: 01874 625515

Beacons Discovery Tours, Glebe Farm, Llanbedr, Crickhowell. Tel: 01873 812144 or email: beacontour@aol.com

Brecon Beacons Mountain Centre, Near Libanus, Brecon LD3 8ER. Tel: 01874 623366

The Brecon Beacons Park Society, c/o Mr. R.T. King (Treasurer/Secretary), 60 Chapel Road, Abergavenny, NP7 7DS

Bibliography

Stone and Steam in the Black Mountains by David Tipper. Published by Blorenge Books

Mid Wales Companion by Moira K Stone. Published by Anthony Nelson Ltd.

Hills and Vales of the Black Mountain District by Richard Baker-Gabb. Published by Jakeman and Carver, Printers

Portrait of the Brecon Beacons by Edmund J Mason. Published by Robert Hale

The Brecon Beacons National Park by Roger Thomas. Published by Webb and Bower

Brecon Beacons National Park (National Park Guide No. 5) edited by Margaret Davies. Published by Her Majesty's Stationery Office

The Story of Brecknock by Wendy Hughes. Published by Gwasg Carreg Gwalch

By the same author:

Circular Walks in Gower

Gwasg Carreg Gwalch
Price: £4.50

Also, **Beacon of Light** – a photographic study of the Brecon Beacon National Park, published by D.W. Jones.